# CHAPTER ONE

# LIFE AND DEATH AT ST. JOSEPH'S

# BARNABY SMITH

a novel

by Daniel Martin Eckhart

Dedicated to those who dare

you can trust me'.

Just then a metallic voice confirmed the appointment, explained where she was to park and wished her a pleasant day. She kept smiling at the camera, nodded, started the car engine and waited. The gate would open, any moment now. It would open and she would be a doctor again … if all went well. She stared at the gate, willed it to open, ready for it to open. When it did, a tremor shot through her and her feet felt alien – the car lurched forward. The engine died.

Damn you, Martha, don't mess this up!

She smiled back at the camera once more, everything's okay, it's not me, it's just the old car, it's not me. Willing herself to breathe, she turned the key again. The Mercedes shot forward, too fast, way too fast. She watched the gate close behind her as she drove up to the main building.

While the hospital itself had a stern, red-bricked Victorian look to it, the grounds were the pure opposite, Martha thought. The park grounds were wide open, dotted with brightly colored flower beds, blossoming trees, white benches – and patients accompanied and watched by attentive nurses.

As she drove to her designated parking spot, she

noticed more cameras, security everywhere … and then she noticed him.

She drove past as if in slow-motion. The patient, dressed in white hospital clothes, sat in the middle of a patch of lawn. Everything about him seemed odd and Martha had seen her share of odd in her thirty years as a psychiatrist. The man appeared to be in his mid-fifties, he was bearded, scarred and wore a knitted cap. She couldn't put her finger on what it was.

The fact that he didn't move as he kept staring into the sky? Or was it the elderly Indian nurse seated right behind the man, servant-like?

Martha's mind snapped back as she almost drove off the road.

Focus on getting this job, Martha.

Tree leaves sparkling in the sun light. Sparrows playing in the wind, chasing each other. Patients walking, sitting, some animated, most in a state of unnatural calm. The peace of sedation, Martha thought. She willed herself to get out of the car, to grab her briefcase, to put on that face again. As she locked the car, her glance went back to the man seated in the grass.

He had not moved. He was still looking up and her eyes followed his gaze. There was nothing up there aside from a few cotton clouds. No, there was something more. She shielded her eyes against the sun, squinted and suddenly saw it.

Way up there, a bird.

It was gliding with the currents, just circling, circling. Martha felt herself pulled into the circle, a hypnotic pull.

She lost her balance, stumbled back against the car and quickly steadied herself once more.

A quick glance.

Nobody's noticed, Martha.

She furtively took a blue lacquered box from her coat pocket, opened it, shaking fingers got hold of a pill. She swallowed it as she put the box away.

A final glance to the man in the grass, unchanged. She didn't dare look up again. The man would sit, the bird would circle, and Dr. Martha Lewis would go get a job.

She took a deep breath and strode purposefully toward the entrance. She didn't want the job, she needed it. Once more she swallowed the desperation that had tried to kill her for the past six months.

Walk in, Martha, walk in and make them believe that you're okay.

# NOTES FROM HIS DIARY

Even then I felt everything. Despite the drugs. For all intents and purposes I was considered catatonic, a vegetable. All for my own safety, of course. Like a doll I was dressed and fed and moved around. I didn't blame them. How could they know that I was alive in there. Mind you, my thoughts weren't clear, but I felt. I felt so much.

I registered the skies and the clouds, I registered the birds and the people. I registered the wind on my cheeks, on the back of my hands, on my fingertips. It was a time I thought would never change again and, I admit, I was content.

Pumped full of drugs I was safe inside my body. Like a thick cocoon made of layers of finest down, in there, protected from the past. I was safe from distant memories, safe from the faces that had made me scream. Silent screams, of course. I don't know why I was aware. I've always been different and I've always been entirely fine with it. Society doesn't like different. Society feels the need to make sense. Everything and everyone needs to fit into a clearly labeled box on a dedicated shelf.

My box? Psychiatrists most often settled on varying

degrees of autism. Most put me into the box marked Asperger's. People with Asperger's Syndrome "are obsessively interested in a single object or topic. They often learn all about their preferred subject and discuss it nonstop. Their social skills, however, are markedly impaired, and they are often awkward and uncoordinated."

Well, I do see their point but why do they have to label everything? The simple fact is that, yes, I am different. My thoughts, my dreams, my mind. Not better or worse, just different. Our happiness lies in this difference, in the thing that defines us, that makes us unique … different is good.

When Martha arrived that day, I saw her. I felt her. I don't know why. To this day, I don't know how. I felt her presence, her desperation. I didn't know what it meant. I certainly didn't know that she would change everything.

After all, I was just a vegetable.

# THE MAN WITH THE BOW TIE

The office of Dr. Charles Richards was, in every way, a reflection of the Charles Martha had met many years ago during their studies. Everything in here was authentic, carefully chosen, lovingly tended. The framed certificates on the walls were simple facts. Charles had never needed to brag. A brilliant mind, a caring friend and, for a short and carefree while, a surprisingly inventive lover, too.

They sat opposite each other in high-backed armchairs, surrounded by books and paintings, steaming cups of tea set before them. He was fifty years old, her age – and he still looked handsome, grey temples, signature bow tie and all.

"I'm glad you're here," Charles said.

"So am I," Martha replied.

She saw that he was watching her, the way she sat, the way she moved. Don't cross your arms, relax your fingers, hold on to his gaze. Smile, Martha, smile. The smile she mustered seemed to stretch across her face with a glowing banner that proclaimed 'Liar, liar, liar!'. Charles smiled back. He didn't seem to notice. He seemed genuinely happy to see her.

"How long has it been?"

"Since we …," Martha said, stopping herself.

"Studied together," Charles added with a playful wink.

Let's not do this. I don't want to do this. Just give me the job, Charles.

"How long? … A very long time, Charles."

He nodded thoughtfully and Martha could see him trying to assess her, read her. She took the cup of tea, blew, sipped and took her time to glance around the office once again. She loved it. She loved this office. As much as she had loved this man once.

There was a statue by the window – the one thing that jarred with everything else in here. Everything was settled, solid, hearth, home … but not that statue of a ferocious looking cast-iron eagle, wings spread wide.

"You like it?" Charles asked.

"No," she said without hesitation. "It isn't you."

He nodded almost mournfully.

"How are you, Martha?"

"I'm fine," she replied, too fast. Slow down, Martha, slow down. "It's, it's been difficult. But I am ready."

"And how is your husband. John, is it?"

"He's all right. Coping. Tell me about St. Joseph's, Charles."

"You don't want to talk about what happened."

"No, I don't." Martha put down the cup of tea, focused on Charles and didn't blink as she continued. "It has been six months since Thomas killed himself. Six months of nothing I would wish on anyone. No. I do not want to talk about my husband or any other part because I have dealt with it. Therapy and all. I am ready to move on."

Charles looked at her for a long moment. With a nod he rose, adjusted his bow tie in the way Martha remembered and asked if she'd like to see the hospital.

~

As they strolled, side by side, through the hallways of St. Joseph's, Martha noticed that she didn't have to fake the smiles anymore. She loved what she saw and it was obvious just how proud Charles was of what was being done here.

They saw and met patients, some smiling, some brooding, some hyperactive and some near comatose. Martha watched Charles interact with the staff, exchange smiles with nurses. He showed Martha every part of the facilities – she saw lively community rooms, a wood shop, a greenhouse – even a music recording studio.

"I like it," Martha said as they walked back toward his office.

"We do our best," Charles said, glowing.

"… Do I get the job?"

"St. Joseph's has two hundred and sixty-seven patients right now," Charles began. "Many with criminal histories. Schizophrenia, delusional disorder, borderline personalities – many of them are dangerous, to others, to themselves."

He had stopped and was now looking down at her. When they were students she had loved the fact that he was this tall – right this moment it annoyed her, more than annoyed her.

It made her angry. She felt like punching him. Instead she just stood and waited, just looked at him.

Make your move, Charles.

"Of course you get the job," he said with a broad smile. "Our mission isn't to keep them in here, it is to see them get well, to leave and become part of life again, out there. And you are one of the best, Martha. St. Joseph's needs you and you'll start on Monday … if that isn't too early for you."

He formally, awkwardly, held out his hand.

For an instant Martha just stared at the hand, then up at him again. Screaming on the inside. Yes! Seemingly calm, she returned the smile and shook his hand.

"Can I start today?"


## PATIENT NUMBER ONE

Martha stood in a barren office, a stack of patient files on a desk, empty shelves along the walls, a high ceiling, a single window. That's where she stood, looking out, looking up. She had the job, the position she had so desperately wanted. She didn't think about it. Empty, like those shelves.

Dark clouds pushed white and blue out of the sky. If the circling bird was still up there, she couldn't see it anymore. She spotted the patient she had seen earlier. He wasn't sitting in the grass anymore. With a heavy limp he ever so slowly made his way toward the building, followed by the Indian nurse. The word 'symbiosis' floated across Martha's mind as a knock on the door gave her a start.

Charles entered, took in the room and the stack of files. He grinned.

"You asked for it."

"Yes, I did."

"You can take your pick," Charles said as he adjusted his bow tie and proceeded to sweep his fingers across the shelves. When he didn't discover any dust, he gave himself a satisfied nod. "But don't overdo it. Start with twelve cases, no more."

"Yes, Sir."

Surprised at her military tone, he looked up only to see her smiling at him. He returned the smile and Martha suddenly realized that this man found her attractive after all these years. A life, a life with Charles, a new life. Stop, Martha. She turned away.

"Who's that?" she said, pointing down to the park grounds.

Charles stepped next to her and she saw instant apprehension, in his movements, in his face, in the way he looked at her and not at her.

"That's Barnaby Smith. He's been here for the past twenty-three years."

"Why?"

"Because he wants to fly."

"He wants to fly?"

"Yes. He wants to fly. Like a bird." He waved his

hand across the window as if to wipe Barnaby Smith away. "You don't want his case."

"Why don't I want his case?"

She saw him squirm and something told her to let it go. Trust Charles. You don't want this case. But something else remembered the bird in the sky, that moment, that hypnotic moment. Her eyes narrowed as Charles struggled to continue.

"Barnaby is with us because he has jumped off roofs nine times in his life."

She stared from Charles to Barnaby Smith and back again.

"And you think this is a problem for me because my son committed suicide by jumping off the roof of a building?" Her voice was hard, harder than she had meant it to be.

"Yes," Charles admitted.

Down there, Barnaby Smith kept limping forward, his gaze empty. A few sparrows landed near him. He stopped and watched until the nurse took his arm and led him on.

"Nine times."

"There isn't a bone he hasn't broken."

"He survived."

"Well, obviously, true. But you really shouldn't -"

"I want his case."

"Martha …"

She turned to look at him, feeling a fire in her eyes, afraid she might burn her old friend but she couldn't help it. Just like she needed this job, she needed Barnaby Smith. The man who had survived when her son had not. Nine times. Nine times! A wail rose deep within her as she remembered looking down from the edge of the roof, down to the sidewalk where people stood and ran and screamed, where a teenage boy lay in a pool of blood, broken, forever broken. Calm down, Martha, calm down.

"Charles, I want his case."


## FLYING WITH THE EAGLES

It was a white room, clean and free of hard edges. A bed, a sink in the corner, a barred window and a richness of pictures on the wall. Birds of every kind and all of them in flight. Owls, hoopoes, egrets, falcons, parrots and pigeons soared as Barnaby Smith, guided by his Indian nurse, entered the room as if sleep-walking.

The elderly nurse gently but efficiently changed Barnaby into his pajamas, brushed his teeth and finally tucked him in as he had done countless times before.

"A lovely day today, wasn't it?" the nurse said.

Barnaby's eyes remained open, blankly staring at the ceiling.

"That bird we saw, Barnaby, you remember seeing that bird?"

The nurse held Barnaby's hand and watched the face closely. It was a game and a constant challenge – trying to connect with Barnaby through the dense fog of medication. At the mention of the word 'bird' there seemed to have been a flicker.

"That bird was not from around here," the nurse continued. "I am not an expert like you but I believe that was an eagle. What is an eagle doing here?"

Barnaby lightly turned his head and looked at the nurse.

"Really?" the nurse said as if answering Barnaby. "You think it was here because of you? That's a nice thought. A very nice thought for a very nice dream."

Barnaby's face didn't change and yet, there was something, a hint of emotion. The nurse smiled, took the knitted cap off Barnaby's head and put it on the night stand. He gently straightened Barnaby's hair and brushed his cheek.

"Fly with the eagles, Barnaby."

A twitch at the side of Barnaby's mouth. Maybe a nerve, the nurse thought. Maybe a smile, he hoped. The moment he rose, Barnaby closed his eyes. The moment he turned off the lights and walked out, Barnaby Smith seemed deep asleep.

## NOTES FROM HIS DIARY

I like quiet. I like solitude, always have. That made me an introvert at best. For some I was a loner and they frowned when I passed in silence and wondered what I was doing in my apartment. Others would whisper to each other, gravely concerned, about the dangers that might come from a stranger they didn't understand. I never minded and they left me alone – for the most part. Of course, when you're the neighborhood weirdo, you do get beaten up occasionally.

St. Joseph's was a blessing, really. I couldn't remember the past and the fully medicated years left me in a state of unchanging peace. It allowed me the time to breathe, to meditate, to explore my mind, to focus on that one thing. Most at St. Joseph's just tried to help and help meant I had to be protected from myself. There were those who were more zealous, those who tried to heal me. Those instances always ended in pain for both sides. But eventually they were satisfied to just contain me, and so was I.

Plus, there was Bharad. A few people have mattered in my life. Just a few. None more than Bharad. I don't know how it happened. I would have called it coincidence at that time … today I think it was meant to be. As a fresh patient, I was assigned to him and from that day on, over the course of twenty-three years, he was always there for me through ... everything. Why would anyone do that? How could anyone be that best of friends when nothing was ever returned?

Sometimes I wish I could just speak. A long time ago I could, when I wasn't a loner, when I was with them and they were with me. When I laughed out loud. The words won't come anymore and so I write them down.

I worry and I shouldn't. I will fly. I feel it. Like a bird, I can sense the change in the air before it happens. Everything is connected, everything from the deepest spaces of my mind to the child that loses a balloon. As the orb rises, as it displaces the air, I can feel it. Like the bird that feels the change even before the wind reaches its wings. It's beautiful. The pressure of the air, just right, the lifting force beneath the wings, that perfect flow.

We don't need feathers or hollow bones or wings of any kind. We can fly. It has happened before, to others, many times. I've been so close to that perfect flow. I was almost there, leaving the ground, more than once.

I felt it.

# A LIFE OF SUICIDE

Martha was exhausted. The day, meeting Charles again, St. Joseph's, the job, trying to balance it all, control it all. The past six months had been a single nightmare and she knew she wasn't ready.

There were times when she dreamed of her son Thomas, there were times when he was with her in broad daylight. When she saw him, when he talked to her. Like he used to, friendly, smiling, but now with the wisdom of the dead. She had gone through therapy, she had done everything suggested and prescribed – everything she herself would prescribe. But it didn't get better. Tommy remained and with it remained the wish to be with him. It would be so easy. If he had done it, so could she. She knew all the ways.

She looked around the apartment she had been in for the past four months. There was no life in here, the many boxes, most still packed, the new furniture still wrapped in plastic. She sat at a coffee table, microwave dinner before her, surrounded by cases files.

Sliding the leftovers aside, she focused on the files again. From the corner of her eye she could see that one thick file named 'Barnaby Smith'. It lay ,separately, untouched. Martha looked at it for a long time and saw the man sitting in the grass again.

Nine times. He had jumped nine times and survived. Martha reached for the file, opened it as if it were fragile. It contained faded psychiatric evaluations, police reports, witness statements, medication charts. A separate manila envelope held a stack of photographs and as they spilled out onto the coffee table, Martha began to glimpse the life of Barnaby Smith.

She looked at the glaringly white living room wall. Office supplies. Somewhere here there was a box that contained office supplies. A sudden surge of energy shot through her as she tore open box after box until she finally discovered what she needed – a small jar full with pins of every color.

She took the first of Barnaby's pictures and pinned it in the center of the wall. It was a black and white photograph of a small boy standing outside what appeared to be an orphanage, the boy's eyes fixed on something in the sky, his mouth open, gaping, lost in wonder. Martha continued pinning images and soon her wall became a most unusual, wildly colorful collage of moments. Here a photograph of a young boy brightly smiling as he showed the wings of a dead pigeon. There a picture of a young man, the face already scarred, the nose broken. Some pictures where snapshots, some portraits. Sometimes Barnaby would ignore the camera, sometimes he appeared to be shy and just rarely did he simply hold still, his quiet intensity fixed on the camera. With every photograph Martha discovered more of Barnaby and continued to pin them, one by one, eagerly, hurriedly – as if the completed panorama of pictures would explain it all.

She froze when something completely unexpected revealed itself. There was young Barnaby, looking somber … and next to him a small young woman with a glowing smile. She was clearly pregnant. Then a wedding picture, followed by another with Barnaby and the woman, now carrying a baby. Martha found herself smiling, felt the warmth of family, the love of parenthood … she was completely unprepared for the next pictures.

Scenes from Barnaby's jumps. Martha saw the tall buildings, saw the marked spots where Barnaby had hit the ground, saw the outlines, blood on the pavement. The photographs seemed to pull her in. The buildings, the height, she rocked back and forth, more and more unsteady as wind rushed in her ears, louder and louder. She felt herself falling, rushing toward the ground, and crashing into the sidewalk with a sickening thud. The last thing she saw was her son, dead, always dead.

Martha woke with a wail. She sat up straight, stared around her. She had fallen asleep on the couch. Barnaby's file around her, photographs on the wall. She sucked in the air, tried to make sense as the sobbing continued. Feverishly, she grabbed for her pill box, opened it with shaking fingers, the pills scattering across the floor. She buried her face in her hands, shaking uncontrollably.

"Stop, Martha, damn you, stop!" she yelled, but the sobbing continued.

~

When Martha woke the next morning, her first thought was of Barnaby Smith. She noticed the sun shining through the little bathroom window.

Freezing. She realized she was curled in the bathtub, the water ice-cold. Must have fallen asleep, cried yourself to sleep, Martha. She had been there before. When she rose, she did her best to ignore the pills and razor blades laid ready on the chair.

## ELEVEN YEARS

Work was good. It kept the demons at bay. On Martha's second day, she gave everyone the feeling that Dr. Charles Richards had hired the perfect woman for the job. She went out of her way to get to know everyone from her peers to the nurses. By day three she had all the names down pat, including cleaning and cafeteria staff. In consultations with her colleagues she was insightful yet humble. And of the twelve cases assigned to her two began to improve right away. By day four she had gone through all of Barnaby's files twice and had a notebook filled with thoughts and ideas.

Time had come to take on patient number one. Martha knocked, didn't wait and stepped into Dr. Henry Steward's office. The middle-aged bearded man rose from behind his desk with a thin smile.

"Dr. Steward, may I have a moment of your time."

"Of course," he said and clearly didn't feel like giving it. Steward stepped around his desk to shake hands and offered her a seat. Martha noticed that the man's eyebrows seemed permanently raised behind his glasses. Martha looked around the office. Everything in here seemed as stiff as the man himself. And, judging from the framed family portrait on the desk, stiffness ran in the family. He had been away at some congress but she'd heard her new colleagues talk about him. Steward was a professional, yes, but also a man who considered himself more so than anyone else here.

"You're German, I take it," he said.

"I've given up trying to lose the accent," Martha simply replied. She had come to the US as a student and had quickly felt more at home here in New York than she ever had in Hamburg. With her degrees and connections, she had found it easy to stay. A flourishing career had followed and then she had met John. They had been happy, so happy. The child, Thomas, completed the picture … until it had all died. The only thing that remained of the old world was the accent.

"Keep it. It gives you a touch of Freud." She smiled and said nothing. "You're here because of Barnaby."

"Yes."

"A very interesting case."

"He has been under heavy sedation for a very long time," Martha said.

"Eleven years," Steward said simply.

"Eleven years." Martha just looked at him and noticed him getting uncomfortable. He took the glasses off his nose and cleaned them on his vest.

"Look, Martha – it is Martha, isn't it?" Steward said. "I know exactly what you're going through."

Martha felt herself stiffen but he seemed too self-absorbed to notice.

"You're new," he continued. "You want to make a difference. And I can assure you, you will. We can help most of our patients at St. Joseph's."

"But not Barnaby Smith?"

Steward leaned forward, took a deep breath and put the glasses back on. His eyebrows rose and when he spoke he spoke as if addressing a child.

"You've read his file. When I came here, I tried all I

could - we all have. For a full two years we experimented. But every time we medicated differently, every time he became aware of his environment, he turned violent."

"He tried to escape," Martha prompted.

"No," Steward replied. "He attempted to commit suicide. Seven times under my care."

"I see."

"I hope you do," he continued. "We do great things here at St. Joseph's. But we cannot help everyone. All we can do for Barnaby is to keep him safe."

## NOTES FROM HIS DIARY

If you want to fly you need to be certain. You need to trust yourself, trust the faculties of your mind. Uncertainty will kill you. When Martha walked into St. Joseph's, she was all uncertainty. Not that she was trying to fly and yet, she was trying. Trying to live again. I admit, I was of no great help.

I felt her around me then, like a cold wind. She was watching me, from the door, across the room, from her office window. I knew she was wondering about my case, about me. How was it possible that I was alive after nine jumps when every one of them should have meant certain death. Certainty. That's why. I never just jumped and I never just fell – I am alive because I flew, even if only for the briefest of moments. I am alive because I willed myself to fly. That kind of talk – and the jumps, of course – were the reasons why everyone thought I was a perfect candidate for St. Joseph's.

At first, when they allowed me to speak, I did my best to explain. But I only had one thing on my side, and that was the fact that I was alive. And as there was no reasonable explanation for it, the rational minds put it aside and filed it under "freak luck" … nine times. Hard to argue with bright minds … when those minds are small.

There can be no understanding until small minds are willing to grow. They never listened to me, not really. They never tried to understand what I was telling them. Eventually I stopped trying. Twenty-three years in that place, going in circles. Everything would repeat itself, over and over again. I had no hope when Martha came, and yet I could feel a change in the air. Today, now, I know that Martha's different. She doesn't believe. But even now her mind is ever so much more open than it used to be. Maybe she'll believe one day. Maybe she'll fly with me.

For some people the world is perfectly clear. They have a ready explanation for everything, making life small, contained, safe. I've always been the opposite. I've always wanted to know what else was out there. If something was put aside as myth, as laughable, as impossible, my mind smiled and explored with the almighty "what if". What if the impossible was possible? What if myth was reality? What if …

There once lived a boy named Giuseppe in the south of Italy, the village of Cupertino. Historical accounts draw the picture of a poor boy, with an equally poor mind – and a unruly temper to go with it. This strange boy, often absent-minded, was given to fits of ecstasy. He experienced visions and was accepted nowhere. Despite his strong interest in religion, the Franciscan monks rejected him twice as his feeble mind and strange behavior made him unfit for tasks as simple as doing the dishes. When, after years of trying, the Franciscans finally admitted him as a stable hand, he began to fly.

It is one of those impossible stories – also one of the best documented ones. Giuseppe spent his time in prayer, ate like a hermit and more and more people took note of his levitations. He would lift stone statues and crosses into the air, he would fly within churches and across fields. Giuseppe, today known as Saint Joseph of Cupertino, became talked about across Europe and his flights were witnessed by hundreds of people, by dukes, by bishops, by cardinals, even by Pope Urban VIII.

Today they call his story just another myth. Science tells us that man cannot fly. The Church has always been cautious when it came to sainthood. What they called miracles had to be witnessed and confirmed. Saint Joseph has been confirmed multiple times, as have many other saints. Of course he flew. But most wouldn't believe what I believe. I would just ask them to consider the possibilities. What if. What if it had happened? Was it a gift of God? Was it religious ecstasy?

What if that young man, five hundred years ago, had experienced seizures instead? What if his mind was active and connected in ways no one could comprehend? What if prayer gave him the mental stability of meditation?

What if he simply flew?

# THE BIRDMAN'S FRIEND

Symbiosis. There it was again, that word. She stood in the shadow of the main hospital building, watching Barnaby and his nurse. People walked past, recognized her. She gave them a thin smile and a curt hello. She didn't want to be seen. She wanted to be left alone to watch Barnaby as he sat in his usual spot in the grass.

Barnaby Smith. Why are you alive? Why are you alive and my son is dead? His face was as blank as she'd come to know it – wiped clean by drugs. Yet his head was tilted to the clouds and his eyes were wide open. As clouds passed and birds crossed his line of vision, nothing happened. No movement, no smile, no reaction of any kind. And still he somehow seemed ... there, taking it in.

She suddenly felt eyes on her and noticed that Barnaby's nurse had spotted her. The expression of the Indian man wasn't unfriendly, he seemed guarded, inquisitive ... protective. Forty-five minutes later, after Barnaby had been handed over to physical therapy on the third floor, the nurse sat in Martha's office. He smiled at her and she felt a sadness, the little man carrying the weight of the world somehow. His name was Bharad Kadam and he had been employed at St. Joseph's for more than thirty years.

"How does that make you feel?" Martha said and Bharad smiled.

"If you don't mind me saying so, you do sound like a psychiatrist."

Caught, she returned the smile.

"What I meant was, you must look forward to retirement after ... how many years?"

"I have been here for thirty-six years. I would like to stay. I am not ready to retire."

"What are you going to do?"

"Do? I will visit Barnaby, every day. Except for Mondays and Tuesdays, of course. There are no visitors allowed on Mondays and Tuesdays." He said it with absolute assurance.

Martha realized that she wasn't taking notes anymore. It didn't matter. A voice in the back of her head told her that she shouldn't be here, that she wasn't a professional, that she should open the window and jump. End it. She kept smiling and Bharad frowned.

"Dr. Lewis?"

"I'm sorry," she said, snapping back. "How long have you been assigned to Barnaby Smith?"

"Since he came here. He's not my only charge, of

course. But I have always been with Barnaby ... and he with me."

"Tell me about him."

"You have not read his file?"

"Tell me something that is not in the file."

Bharad looked at her in confusion but saw that she was entirely serious. He thought for a moment, then nodded lightly.

"My full name is Bharadwaj. It is the name of one of our most revered gurus. It is also the name of a bird. And I was given the care of the birdman."

"... You think that you and Barnaby Smith were - meant to meet?"

Bharad shrugged.

"He is my friend, and I am his," he replied. "I am afraid that what I am telling you will not be of much help in your psychiatric evaluation."

Lost in the man's kindness, a forgotten warmth. Martha put on a smile and pretended to make a note.

"Thank you for your time," she said.

He stood up, lightly bowed and then, at the door, turned back to her.

"I have known him before the medications, Dr. Lewis. I know Barnaby. And I have never met anyone like him in my life." Martha, Barnaby's file open before her, looked up at Bharad as he continued. "They used to ask him, all the time, 'Why do you want to fly, Barnaby?'"

"And he would reply," Martha added, her hand on the file, "Why do you want to breathe?"

Bharad nodded as if this would explain everything.


## SOMEWHERE IN THERE

Martha had been unable to find any information about Barnaby Smith's life before the age of five. Until then, all that had been recorded was his discovery on the steps of orphanage. Did something happen between then and his first jump?

It was a crystal-clear day, the 17th of June, when five-year-old Barnaby climbed onto the roof of the orphanage wearing a blue cape and a big smile. The nuns spotted him but all their shouting, threatening and praying didn't help.

A letter from one of the nuns was in Barnaby's file. She maintained that she had never seen a happier boy than Barnaby Smith. Glowing as he spread his arms, joyous as he jumped forward, blissful as he fell. In her letter, the nun described the moment of the falling boy in great detail, the fluttering cape, the boy's hair, ruffled by the wind. She wrote that 'The boy's arms, all the way to his fingertips, were stretched wide. He was not afraid. I don't understand it. I will never understand it. That boy was not afraid. He believed that he was flying.'

After that first jump, a jump he barely survived, a lot of notes were taken. Barnaby was observed, evaluated and eventually deemed no longer a threat to himself or others. He was an odd boy, certainly, but never a burden. He smiled a lot, kept to himself and didn't seem to mind being bullied again and again. His interests were elsewhere.

~

Barnaby Smith sat in a small meeting room. He stared straight ahead and gave no indication that anything around him reached his brain. Martha sat opposite him, together with Dr. Steward. She didn't want Steward here but for this first interaction he had insisted on being present, after all, Smith had been his patient. In the corner behind Barnaby stood Bharad, watching her, watching Steward.

Martha focused on Barnaby. The man was fifty-four years old, scars across his face, some hidden by the scruffy beard. From the files, she knew that his nose had been broken at least eleven times. And not just his nose – skull and jaw fractures over the years had dented this face considerably. Martha struggled to discover even a hint of that blissfully glowing boy the nun had described in her letter so many years ago.

Those eyes, the color of sunlit sky just before the storm. Please, Martha thought, please, there has to be life left in there somewhere.

"My name is Dr. Martha Lewis. I am here to help you."

If he heard her, he didn't show it. With everything she knew about his medication, she couldn't expect a reaction. She knew that Steward, impatiently sitting next to her, thought this a complete waste of time. Barnaby didn't move, looked at the wall behind her, looked through it. His hands were flat on his thighs, his feet parallel and his posture surprisingly straight for a man who'd broken so many bones so many times.

"I have read about the accident, Barnaby. I am very sorry for the loss of your wife and daughter. You remember the accident."

She had intended to rattle him with the car accident that had killed Barnaby Smith's wife and child. The accident that had occurred just shortly before his ninth jump, before being committed to St. Joseph's for good. But Barnaby's face remained unchanged, no flicker of memory, not a twitch, nothing. Steward turned to her, opened his mouth to speak but Martha signaled him to remain silent. From the corner of her eye she saw how displeased he was. Good. She tried again.

"Barnaby ... why do you want to fly?"

Steward sighed loudly and tried to rise. Martha grabbed his arm and pulled him back down, her eyes on Barnaby. There was something, she had seen something.

"Wait," she whispered, before addressing Barnaby again. "Why do you want to fly?"

Slowly, ever so slowly, Barnaby's hands began to float off his thighs. They hovered just a few inches above his legs and swayed lightly, as if they were wings floating on the wind. Martha stared at the hands as if they were magical – and the magic continued when she saw Barnaby's face. He was smiling.

"I cannot stop you from making my mistakes, Martha," Steward said. He was clearly frustrated as he looked from her to the smiling Barnaby and back. "But I do implore you – do not lower his medication. You are not helping him."

Martha said nothing. She gave Bharad a nod and left the room.

## NOTES FROM HIS DIARY

I remember the day of our first meeting. Martha was there and so was my dear friend Dr. Steward. He was his usual self, a mind constantly struggling to keep the world exactly the same. Steward was responsible for varying degrees of pain during my years in his care but I bear no ill will toward him. Besides, I vaguely remember punching him more than once when he played around with the drug dosages. It wasn't personal. My body reacts to drugs, or lack thereof, as does everyone else's.

Martha mentioned my wife and daughter. I hadn't thought of them in years. Their faces had vanished behind the clouds. It was the strangest sensation to see them slowly come into focus again, to catch glimpses of a life filled with love, life as a husband, life as a father. I didn't remember the details. That came later, the screaming came later. I just saw Martha, her unblinking eyes, intensely focused.

And I heard her voice. "Why do you want to fly?"

It took all my strength to move my hands, to lift my fingers, to make them float. I knew she wouldn't be able to help me, but I felt her pain. From that first moment, I knew that she was special, both weak and strong. And so, I floated my hands. A signal to tell her that she wasn't alone. That there was hope, life. If not for me, for her.

Looking at her back then, I knew what she wanted to do. The same as everyone else had done before her. It was senseless, and I knew that it was just another part of the never-ending cycle that was life at St. Joseph's. She would try and she would fail. I was convinced of it and I wasn't mad about the inevitability of what was to come.

Now, weeks later ... so much has happened. Martha. Sometimes an act of desperation is exactly what's required.

# TEARS AND COFFEE

Why. Why this job? Why Barnaby? Why was she here, still here? Why did a fifteen-year-old boy kill himself? Barnaby Smith had given a sign of life, a sign of willpower that had pushed through eleven years of complete sedation. And maybe it was nothing. Wishful thinking. The same old weakness that forced her to cling to her miserable excuse of a life. The same old pathetic thought that somehow, it would all make sense again.

She pushed through the door of the staff lounge, relieved to find no one there. The room was cozy with sofas and bean bag seats, a high-end coffee machine and large plants. Martha ignored it all as she stood by the window, crying. She didn't turn around when the door opened.

"Oh, hi Martha, staff meeting in five." Charles' voice.

"I'll be there," she said, not turning around.

She heard Charles walking in, grabbing a mug, pushing a button. The screech of coffee beans. She turned away even more and pretended to stretch, trying to wipe her tears in the process. Coffee in hand, Charles stepped next to her and looked out the window.

"Beautiful day."

"Yes."

"I have to tell you, your colleagues are greatly impressed with the progress some of your - … Martha? Are you all right?"

She turned to him, trying to look strong but she knew he could tell. There was nothing uncertain about her red eyes.

"I'm fine, Charles. It's just … sometimes …"

"I understand."

Do you, Charles? Martha thought, anger suddenly tearing at her insides. Do you really? Have you watched your son die? Do you carry razor blades in your pockets, just in case you can't take it anymore?

Charles kept looking at her, with that deep concern in his eyes. She couldn't bear it anymore and hurried off.


## THE DREAM OF FLIGHT

Human beings had always dreamed of flight. For two thousand years that dream had been one of flying like the birds, with feathers and flapping wings. Every attempt a failure and, most often, a death. From the legend of Icarus to the early medieval tower jumpers, from moors to monks and from Leonardo da Vinci to Otto Lilienthal, the German birdman pioneer who completed over two thousand flights with his gliders before a sudden gust of wind killed him.

It was late night as Martha stepped back from her living room wall. More and more of Barnaby's life was pinned there. More photographs, more documents, even a map of the world with many red markers. Places, Martha now knew, Barnaby had visited on his quest to discover the secret of human flight.

A growing part of the wall was given to flight. Traditional flight, flight the way sane human beings attempted to conquer the sky. There was the first hot-air balloon of the Montgolfier brothers and, pinned right next to it, pictures of Amelia Earhart, Lindbergh, Yeager, Armstrong. There were the Wright Brothers with their first flyer at Kitty Hawk. Explorers, adventurers with the courage to go from dreaming to daring.

But none of what they had dared and achieved was Barnaby's dream. His dream was far simpler and hence, impossible. The madness of wanting to fly without aid, to fly, just - like - that.

There wasn't much she found about Barnaby's family. There was that one photograph of Barnaby standing next to his wife, Vanessa. She looked wispy, smiled at the camera. In her arm, the baby girl named Aura. Barnaby and Vanessa stood close.

He didn't smile. From within the picture he looked out at Martha and she felt herself getting pulled into his eyes.

Those eyes of sky. She heard the sound of the wind, rushing, stronger, louder.

Turn away, Martha. Turn away from it all.


## GOOD MEMORIES

Charles had insisted on taking her out for lunch. She had settled in nicely, was working hard, too hard he said, and so here his present, lunch with the boss. The garden restaurant was classy, too classy for lunch with a colleague. Martha knew it, he pretended to be unaware. Charles had never married. 'Never met the right woman?' she had asked him once, off-handed, just a question, not thinking. When he didn't reply and instead just gave her a shrug and a smile, she quickly changed the subject.

What a day. The restaurant didn't have a Brooklyn feel. Trees and potted plants gave a sense of being in the country and the courtyard walls kept out the noise from the street. The sun turned everything into a kaleidoscope of light and dark, shades of leaves playing on Charles' face as he smiled at her.

"You should really try this," he said, finishing his dessert.

"I should get back."

He took a final bite, wiped the corners of his mouth.

"Steward's is not happy," Charles said.

"Maybe he should try medication," Martha said, pushing away her plate.

"Martha, I'm not happy either."

"I am making progress."

"Yes. You've had a big impact with most of your subjects these past three weeks. You being here, with us, is good," he said with that awkward wanting smile of his.

"You shouldn't have brought me to this place."

"Surely two colleagues can enjoy a decent bit of lunch together." Martha just looked at him and his smile gave way to worry lines. "You work day and night."

"I'm not claiming overtime."

"You know what I'm saying."

"Yes I know what you're saying and I've told you, I've dealt with it."

"... You didn't tell me that your husband left you."

She stared at him, felt like hurting him. They had already taken her plate and cutlery. His luck. Something within her wanted to stab that caring look from his eyes. She simply rose and left without another word. Charles sighed and signaled for the check.

~

Charles was quiet behind the steering wheel as they drove back to St. Joseph's. The radio was turned off, the windows up. Silence in the car and Martha was intent on keeping it that way. All she wanted, all she needed, was to work. Leave me alone, Charles.

"Martha ..." he finally said and it sounded like an apology.

"My private life is none of your business."

He stopped the car outside the gates of St. Joseph's. They waited in uncomfortable silence. With the gates finally open, Charles drove on.

"When we studied together -" he started.

"- we were different people."

Martha saw him nodding, not looking at her. Shy. He parked the car in the chief administrator's spot and stayed

48

seated, his hands remaining on the steering wheel. Martha put her hand on his.

"We were young," she added.

"Remember the night in the library?"

"Good memories," she said and her smile was real. She gave his hand a gentle pat and opened the door. She wouldn't be able to handle any more of this kind of conversation. When Charles got out, they looked at each other over the roof of the car.

"I need to get back to work."

"That's what I hired you for," he said, mock-serious.

"Indeed."

Stepping away from the car they saw, among a dozen other patients and nurses, Barnaby and Bharad.

The old Barnaby was gone. This Barnaby was no longer near-catatonic, this Barnaby walked circles, always staring up. Bharad's eyes followed Barnaby's every move.

"I've seen that before, Martha," Charles said. "Another day and you'll have to either medicate or restrain."

"I told you I'm making progress."

"That's what Steward said when he first came to us. Then Barnaby attacked him."

"I can help him."

"Steward?" Charles asked. Martha gave him a smirk and he gladly took it. "Just be careful," he added as he looked at his watch and hurried off.

## NOTES FROM HIS DIARY

I've experimented with drugs – not the synthetic kind, mind you, but with everything shamans have used for thousands of years. When I was free, before meeting Vanessa, I spent every penny on flight. On learning it, learning about it – and meeting with those who knew more than modern man. I went to Siberia, India, Alaska, Japan and many other places to meet wise women and men. Of course, I also met a lot of charlatans, but I never minded them. Even within their jaded minds there was a hidden belief that maybe, just maybe, their hoaxes could be more than that.

I never saw any of them fly. The wisest among them would tell me stories, would show me paths – but most often they were drug-induced trances only, flights of the mind, nothing more. Coming off those trances was often surprising and never, ever, destructive on either mind or body. Coming off the levels of medication at St. Joseph's was an altogether different experience.

When before I was sitting in a cocoon, a safely padded cell of the mind, suddenly those walls would disappear. No more safety. No more peace. I would see, hear and feel everything at once. Too much for any mind – and for one that had been muted for years? Chaos. I would see Bharad but I wouldn't just see him. I would smell what he had had for breakfast and would picture it and crave it. I would see a spot on his aging skin and it would pull me in like a black hole. I would see his smile and I'd feel like hurting him. But there was more than Bharad – there were all the other nurses, patients and doctors. Everyone an explosion of impressions. Everyone a universe of chaos. All around me, all the senses, all the time. I could feel single leaves of grass under my slippers. I would see a beetle and hear six hairy legs scraping along the path.

I'd never wish it on anyone. It is the place where death becomes the only option. As calm as I have always been in my fully medicated bubble, the in-between is something that drove me mad. It made me realize who I was, where I was and just how futile my so-called life had become. A speck of life, no more meaningful than dust. Dust that would fade away in a corner. In those days, the days when Martha experimented on me, I was left with the most painful clarity that there was no escape, no freedom, no flight – ever.

When we met for our next session, I wanted to tell her so much. I wanted to tell her about flight, about belief, about the mind. I wanted to talk to her about Jesus walking on water, about prophets pulled high into the air. I wanted to implore, I wanted to urge her to open her mind, to think about all the stories. I wanted to tell her that human flight had happened, was happening, not just to the special few – that it had happened to saints and children, shamans and farmers, yogis and housewives, mediums and businessmen. I wanted to share with Marta everything that I had ever learned ...

... But that's not what happened. What happened wasn't Barnaby Smith. I wasn't in control, of my mind, of my senses, of my body.

She knew that, she had been warned.

# I WILL KILL YOU

Martha had soon learned a number of things about Barnaby's past. Much of it from transcripts, from a time when Barnaby still spoke. He had clearly been a loner and yet love had come looking for him in the form of a frail looking young woman named Vanessa. She lived across the street from Barnaby and he had never noticed her because his eyes were always trained on birds. From the way Barnaby told it, Vanessa trapped him.

Working at a small pet shop, owned by a French man named Maurice Merlin, Barnaby spent, no great surprise, most of his time in the room-sized birdcage in the back. A room filled with parrots and finches, canaries and parakeets, separated from the rest of the shop with a mesh wire wall. Barnaby's favorite place, surrounded by the sights and sounds of wings in flight. One day, as Barnaby was in the middle of his daily cleaning routine in the cage, he felt the presence of someone else. He turned to see a young woman standing there. He turned away and continued working. When he looked again, a long while later, she was still there. Smiling at him.

Focus on the now, Martha. Now. She was back in the same room where she'd met Barnaby the first time around, the time of his floating hands. It was all different today. Barnaby pacing, Martha the calming presence, seated. Bharad stood nervously in the corner from where he watched Barnaby's every move.

"I know you can hear me," Martha said.

He just kept pacing. No reaction, not a glance, nothing. Martha could see just how rattled he was. She saw his shaking hands, she saw the sweat glistening on his forehead.

"I want to help you," she said. "I can help you - but you have to want it."

The pacing continued, his eyes focused on the ground. Martha was only too aware of the danger. Drawing him out into the clear could go either way. They had all warned her, yet here she was. Anything could happen.

"Tell me about Vanessa."

Still no reaction.

"Tell me about Aura."

Barnaby kept pacing back and forth as before. But Martha caught a glance from Bharad. He looked deeply concerned and shook his head. She ignored him and continued.

"Aura is a lovely name for a girl. I have a feeling you

chose it. Aura - its meaning is wind, isn't it?"

A sudden stop. Barnaby just stood there, staring at his slippers.

Martha looked up at him as he turned to stare down at her. Bharad took a step forward, ready to jump in.

"Who are you?" Barnaby asked, his voice raw and cracked.

"My name is Dr. Martha Lewis. I am here to help you."

"I will kill you."

Martha felt fear rising as Barnaby leaned in closer. She forced herself to stay calm as Bharad stepped in, touching Barnaby's arm, his voice soothing.

"Barnaby, please could you -"

Without turning, without looking at Bharad, as if flicking off an annoying insect, Barnaby's arm swung back, striking Bharad across the head. Bharad flew hard against the wall and slowly sank to the ground, holding his head. Martha pushed the alarm button but stayed in place. Don't escalate. Watch him. He's out now, he's here.

"Why do you want to kill me?" she asked.

"I want my medication."

"No, you don't. You want to be free. You want to

fly." She could see him getting ready to explode and when he did, the agony in his scream shook her.

"I – want – my – medication!"

She heard running, the stomping of heels, she heard the door being unlocked, she saw the guards rushing in and tackling Barnaby. He punched and kicked and kept his eyes on Martha as they grabbed him and ushered him out. Martha looked at her hands.

They were shaking, just slightly. Barnaby Smith had frightened her. But her fear was easily matched by her fascination.

She suddenly rushed to her feet and ran from the room.

## A LIFE FOR BARNABY

Bharad sat in the infirmary on a stretcher, a nurse treating the bruised side of his face. Martha stood by the door and watched him closely. Bharad looked old, she thought, old and weak and … sad. The moment the nurse left the room, Martha stepped in.

"He did not attack you." Bharad looked at her in confusion. "You fell. Bharad, please. Help me help him.

He can have a life, a real life. But if you tell them what happened –"

"I fell," he said.

The nurse returned with fresh gauze and proceeded to bandage Bharad's head. He just let it happen. His eyes remained on Martha and he smiled, wondering.

"A life for Barnaby ... wouldn't that be something."

~

Less than ten minutes later Steward had called for immediate action and urged a meeting to reassess the Barnaby Smith situation. Now here they were, in Charles' office. Charles behind his desk, wearing the cool demeanor of a hospital administrator. Steward stood by the window, his eyebrows in high gear as he glared at Bharad who stood in front of Charles' desk, hands folded before him, looking like a school boy.

Bharad's eyes went from Charles to Martha and back again. Charles gave a light nod and, as Bharad left, Martha sent him a smile that said 'thank you'. With Bharad gone, Steward threw up his hands in frustration.

"He fell, of course," Steward said to Charles, before turning to Martha. "What are you trying to do? I don't see the logic, I don't see the value, I don't see the progress and I particularly don't see how anything you're doing is in any way different from what has been tried several times before."

"There is hope," Martha simply said.

"You pushed the alarm button."

Martha said nothing.

"Why did you push the button?" Charles asked her. She took a moment, as if to collect her thoughts. In fact, she knew exactly what she was going to say. Now she just had to convince Charles to let her continue.

"I am not saying that he currently does not pose a certain risk to himself and those around him – but I need him aware. Fully aware of what's real."

"Real?" Steward said, stepping closer. "Realty is the place where he knows that he will never fly like a bird, the place where, because of that, he wants to kill himself. Reality is the place of certain death for Barnaby Smith."

"We can increase security." She didn't look at Steward, ignored him. Her eyes on Charles only. Come on, Charles. I need this. She saw him wavering, looking from her to Steward and back.

"What do you see, Martha?"

"When I was in that room with him, when I talked to

him about his wife and child … Barnaby focused. He said to me 'I will kill you'."

"Ah yes," Steward said, "Now I see why you're hopeful."

"The man I saw in there was full of rage, but not suicidal. On the contrary. He may not even know it – but Barnaby Smith wants to live." Steward shook his head. Small birds streaked by outside, fast. Swallows? Martha wondered. She saw them coming and going behind Steward. Probably a nest somewhere under the roof. Probably little ones up there, hungry, screaming for food. Tommy. She forced herself back into the conversation.

"He is responsible for the death of his wife and child," Steward said gravely. "He has always been fully conscious of this fact. Their death, his fault. The night after they were buried, he entered the construction site of a 17-story building and jumped from the highest possible point."

"He is only just beginning to appear, Charles. I need time with him, real time. Un-medicated time." She saw Charles considering it, leaning her way. She saw Steward seeing it. She saw Steward shaking his head in utter frustration.

"This is a grave mistake," Steward said.

# I LIKE FLYING, TOO!

Vanessa. In the transcripts, Barnaby left no doubt that he had deeply loved his wife. That he had adored his daughter Aura. That their death had devastated him.

The reason for their coming together was simply and purely Vanessa's persistence. Martha's research showed that Vanessa had been an only child, the daughter of a fireman and a seamstress. Vanessa liked to stare into space when everyone else was talking. Vanessa liked to shout out loud when everyone else was silent in church. Vanessa was wild and vibrant and odd and altogether unlike any of the other girls. Her parents had taken her to see a psychiatrist but he only confirmed what they already knew – there was nothing wrong with Vanessa. She was bright and smart … and she was simply different. Without a doubt, it was that very difference that attracted her to Barnaby.

According to Barnaby's transcripts, she kept watching him and their first conversation occurred one evening as he and Maurice Merlin were closing the shop for the night. Barnaby said goodbye to Merlin, a quick and awkward handshake as always. Merlin walked off in one direction, Barnaby in the other and that's when Barnaby noticed Vanessa standing on the other side of the street. He pretended not to have seen her and walked on, picking up the pace just a little. But as he did, so did she. She crossed the street and walked next to him, friendly, openly, eagerly.

"I'm Vanessa."

As Barnaby walked even faster, she had to half-run to keep up.

"I've been watching you."

"You keep coming to the shop," he said gruffly to get her to stop speaking.

"You're Barnaby. I heard Mr. Merlin call you Barnaby." Maybe she didn't notice that he was highly agitated at this point. "Barnaby. It's a nice name," she brightly said.

"Go away."

"We have the same way home," Vanessa explained. "I live right across from you. You live alone, don't you?" Barnaby abruptly turned a corner into another street. She followed and bounced along next to him.

"Please go away?" Barnaby tried.

"I've seen all the birds and models and things you have at home. Through the window, you know."

Too much to handle. Barnaby turned and ran off, as

fast as his legs would carry him. The last thing he heard, the last words from that first conversation with Vanessa caught up with him, her voice strong and bright as a bell.

"I like flying, too!"


## NOTES FROM HIS DIARY

How often do we act before we think? How much time to we spend on regret? Regrets about the things we did and regrets about the things we didn't do. Most often a pause and a breath make all the difference. Most often we don't take the time for that pause. Most often choices are ours.

That day, the day when I threatened to kill Martha, choice wasn't available to me. Things just happened. I just happened. I remember not fitting into that room. I remember the lack of air. She was there. Martha. Desperate Martha Lewis. And she tried so hard to draw me out of my cocoon and something did come out. Something that wasn't me. Something that hurt the only friend I had.

It's all about connections. Connections with, and into, everything. At the orphanage, they would give us crayons and draw-by-numbers sheets. All we had to do was follow the numbers. One, two, three, four, five … and eventually we'd have the shape of an elephant. I've never enjoyed those drawings. But connecting all the numbers in the right order would create something that made sense. That day, the day when I struck Bharad and scared Martha, none of the connections within me made sense. Everything was wrong.

It was then that my past flooded back into me. With my one quest in life there had been no room for anything else … anyone else. When I met Vanessa, I resisted for as long as I could - until I discovered this new thing … love.

I hated her for that love. I hated her for making me question my singular purpose in life. I hated her for pushing flight from my mind. And I loved her. I loved her so much, her laughter, her courage. I love her, still. My Vanessa, my wife. She was a miracle, as impossible as a rainbow in a living room. And yet there she was, full of light and love and she pulled me in when I had nothing but flight on my mind. She smiled when I tried to ignore her. She smiled when I tried to run.

Love. As impossible as flying. And yet people try again and again. They climb, they jump, they fall, they hurt and they jump again … until they fly. Isn't it surprising that people have no problem believing in love? To me, Vanessa was yet another proof that everything is possible. She chose me. She loved me. And then Aura arrived. The magic of a child. The happiness of family. Who would have thought.

I promised her that I wouldn't try to fly anymore. For her sake, for the sake of the family. I had responsibilities now, as a husband, as a father. Vanessa did everything she could to make our life magical. My love for her and our daughter took my breath away and my promise did the same. It was a full life, a happy life. A life of play and joy … and I couldn't breathe anymore.

I fully expected to be returned to my medicinal cocoon after the outburst. Following that session I waited for the pills to take me back to safety. I wanted to cry and I would laugh. I wanted to speak and I would scream. I wanted to eat and I would spit. I wanted to forget the faces and I couldn't. No one came to mute the chaos. I kept seeing Vanessa, smiling at me. I kept hearing Aura's laughter, bright as a summer song. I kept feeling a life that I couldn't live.

# A NIGHT IN INDIA

Martha stood outside a small apartment building on the edge of Sunset Park. She rang the bell and waited. A nice evening, the air was filled with the sounds of people enjoying spring. People calling their dogs, people laughing with friends, people playing ball, people shouting at neighbors. People with lives.

She tried to tune it all out and rang the bell again. Nothing. She was just about to walk away when the door opened. Bharad stood there, out of breath.

"Dr. Lewis?"

"I'm sorry to disturb you in your spare time, but I –"

"Are you hungry?" he said with a smile and waved her in.

Nice, Martha thought. Warm. She was sitting in Bharad's kitchen. He had served her an excellent curry, too spicy. Everything she had seen in the apartment had an Indian touch. Bharad had been a most attentive host. Now he finally sat opposite her.

"You miss India?" she asked.

"I miss the idea of India. I came here as young man, my family, my children - all here ... somewhere."

"You don't see them much?"

"I have three daughters - doctors like you. Very smart. Very busy. My wife has died many years ago. If I may ask, do you have family?"

"Not anymore," she said. "Dinner was delicious."

Bharad rose, gave her a smile of thanks and put the plates in the sink.

"You are here because of Barnaby," he suggested.

"... You said that you have never met anyone like him in your life. What did you mean by that?" Bharad motioned her to follow and left the kitchen.

"I would like to show you something."

A narrow hallway led to two rooms in the back of the apartment. Martha saw right away that 'India' stopped there – the hallway was all about flight. The framed pictures on the walls showed everything from airplanes to birds and clouds.

"What is all this?" Martha asked.

"Barnaby's things," Bharad replied.

He opened the door to the guest room and waved her inside. Martha stepped into the room and slowly turned. She was stunned, taking it all in. It felt like being inside Barnaby's head. Everything in this room was about flying. There were pictures, drawings and paintings on the walls, the were studies of wings, airplane models and stuffed birds hanging from the ceiling and books upon books on the shelves and stacked wherever the crammed little room allowed.

"They emptied his apartment when Barnaby came to stay with us," Bharad explained. "Mr. Merlin had no room. They, they would have thrown all of this away ..."

"It's beautiful," Martha whispered. Bharad smiled.

"In your profession, one might also call it obsessive, I believe."

He took a blue photo album from the shelf and asked her to take a seat on the worn sofa bed. Bharad gave her the album, encouraging her with a nod to open it. Martha didn't know what to expect but it felt special.

She opened it gingerly as if it were an ancient manuscript that might crumble to dust if handled roughly. It was just a regular photo album. And yet it wasn't. It contained, from the first to the last page, nothing but snapshots of clouds. When she looked up, she saw Bharad gently brushing dust off the feathers of a dove.

"If flying were possible," Bharad said, "just if, it would take a man of Barnaby's determination to accomplish it."

"There are many ways of flying," Martha said.

Bharad nodded and handed her another photo album. When Martha flipped the pages she saw that this album was all about Barnaby's many explorations into flight. She saw him parachute, paraglide, bungy-jump – it was all in here and much of the flying was done together with Vanessa. They looked happy.

"He tried them all," Bharad explained. "Barnaby even has a pilot's license. But what he wants, what he has always wanted, is this. To spread his wings -" Bharad spread his arms wide and rose onto his toes, "- and lift off."

"Is it a bird? Is it a plane? No, it's ..."

"Barnaby," Bharad said, finishing the sentence for her.

Martha smiled.

~

It was late night when Martha left. They had lost the sense of time in Barnaby's world, looking at his pictures, reading through his notes, talking to each other. Martha had felt a comfort, being there, together with Bharad. He believed. She needed to believe. But he simply believed in Barnaby. Bharad accompanied her down the stairs, stepped out into the night with her. She shook his hand.

"Thank you."

"It was my pleasure," Bharad said. Martha saw him hesitate.

"What is it?

"You do believe that Barnaby wants to live."

"Yes," Martha answered without hesitation.

"... I see him looking at the birds," Bharad said pensively. "There is no happiness in his eyes. Please be careful, Dr. Lewis."

"I am," she said and walked off into the darkness. Was she? Careful? Enough? The concern in Bharad's eyes stayed with her deep into her dreams.

## LET ME DIE

Martha and Charles entered the small observation room. From here a one-way mirror allowed an open view into the meeting room on the other side. Barnaby was sitting at the table, grim-faced, locked tight into a straightjacket. Waiting behind Barnaby was an oversized guard and Bharad.

"Oh, come on, Charles."

"You agreed," Charles said, raising his hands in defense as if he expected her to attack him. "Increased security. It's either that or meds."

"Charles, please. How am I supposed to get through to a man who wants to fly if he can't even flap his arms?"

"But we don't want him to flap his arms, do we? We want him to realize that he is a human being and as such is not ever going to fly."

"No straitjacket." Charles sighed, exasperated.

"Why are so you fixated on him?"

"He's an enigma, Charles. Tell me you don't find him fascinating."

"Steward has another theory."

"Of course he does," Martha shot back. "What do you think?"

"I'm not sure," Charles conceded.

"Well, when you are, let me know," Martha said, her hand on the door. "In the meantime, tell them to remove the straight-jacket. I'd like to continue with my work."

Moments later she was in the room, sitting opposite Barnaby. He rubbed his arms, stretched them.

The oversized guard behind Barnaby had the straightjacket next to him on the ground, at the ready. He watched Barnaby uneasily.

Martha and Bharad exchanged a smile – then she focused on Barnaby.

"I'm Dr. Martha Lewis."

"We have met before," Barnaby said, his voice measured.

"Yes."

"Leave me alone."

He sat still, his voice calm. But he wasn't, Martha knew. Couldn't be. Since lowering his medication, Barnaby had been flooded with everything his senses were able to latch on to. His mind and body had been deprived for years – now it was all rushing in, a constant stream of sights and sounds and smells … and thoughts.

Too much thinking can destroy you, Martha. Too much thinking causes sons to commit suicide, Martha.

Too much thinking, too much blood.

Focus on Barnaby, Martha.

"I want to talk about your family," she said.

"I don't," he replied instantly. End of conversation.

"Did you try to commit suicide after the death of your family?"

Barnaby put his hands on the table and leaned forward. He spoke quietly but with great intensity.

"I've done this before," he said. "I don't remember the men before Steward. But they tried. Then he came. He tried. Now you're here."

"Barnaby, if we were to release you today, what would you do?"

He just stared at her, as if willing her to go away.

"Let me help you," she continued.

"Let me die," he softly said.

Martha looked at him, stared at him, hated him.

She was locked in his eyes, couldn't pull herself away. She felt tears forming and forced them back.

You can't die, Barnaby, I'm not going to let you die.

'I'm not going to let you die', she screamed inside her head.

In the room, she blinked and a tear fell and she saw that Barnaby noticed.

He frowned as she took the file and left the room.

~

That night Barnaby brushed his own teeth and Bharad watched it with a smile and hidden concern. Barnaby was awake, alive … but Bharad has seen 'alive' before, it meant danger, grave danger. When Barnaby had put on his pajamas, he climbed into bed and then let Bharad do the rest. Bharad first restrained Barnaby's arms, doing so gently but still making sure it was tight enough to be safe. Barnaby kept his eyes on Bharad, he just let it happen.

"That's a nasty bruise," Barnaby said.

"I fell," Bharad said with a shrug.

"And I'm sorry," Barnaby replied.

Surprised, Bharad realized that Barnaby remembered everything that had happened. Bharad just nodded, pulled the blanket up to Barnaby's chin, tucking him in.

"She is a nice woman," Bharad said. He took off Barnaby's cap, as always, put it on the shelf and gently brushed his cheek. "You should give her a chance. Good night, Barnaby."

Barnaby didn't react in any way. He simply closed his eyes. The guard at the door left. Bharad left. The door closed.

Barnaby opened his eyes.

"Good-bye, my friend," he said gently.

# NOTES FROM HIS DIARY

There's a story that's been with me for many years. I don't recall where I've heard it … a song, perhaps? It is the story of a man who wanted to end his life. All he had wanted, for as long as he could remember, was to end it. But there were his parents and he didn't want them to feel sad. He would bear this strange thing, this life. He waited. Year after year went by and he waited, patiently. And when his father died, his mother passed on shortly thereafter.

With a smile on his face the man left the funeral. His time had come. But when he bought the rope to hang himself with, he bumped into the woman that would soon become his wife. And so he lived, and waited again. He didn't want to cause her pain. Children weren't meant to be, not for lack of trying, and the man was not altogether unhappy about it. A wonderful life it was and in her eighty-third year, his wife passed away. The old man smiled as he felt old sadness rise. It was time. It was finally time.

He walked onto the bridge that had proven to be such an effective suicide spot for many before him. Just as he was about to climb the railing, he heard a soft whimper behind him and there stood a neglected mutt. And so the man talked to the dog and it followed him home. The dog was old and would surely die soon and the man took good care of him – best friends in old age. The man would wait. He had been patient his whole life, he had borne the sadness before, he could do it one more time. After all, he didn't want the dog to be all alone.

One day the old man gently scratched the dog behind the ears, gave him an afternoon snack and made himself comfortable in his rocking chair on the porch. The dog sat next to the old man and together they watched the world pass by until the rocking chair stopped rocking. The old man had died peacefully in his sleep.

I've always felt great sympathy for that man. I've never wanted to commit suicide, although they kept saying it. Every one of my jumps was an attempt to fly. Every one of those attempts was a failure and yet every attempt has brought me a step closer to my goal. Not death, never death. Flight.

But it was different inside St. Joseph's. Despite Martha's attempts I knew that I would never be free to fly.

# INTO FREEDOM

Barnaby and Vanessa sat on the floor of the small plane, packed in between twenty other people, all decked with parachutes, helmets and goggles. The sliding door was wide open, the wind making conversation impossible. Still, one of the instructors was standing and shouting, laughing, entertaining them all. Some were first-time jumpers, some more experienced – it was easy to see the fluttering nerves.

In the conversations that had taken place shortly after being institutionalized at St. Joseph's, Barnaby had spoken about his first jump with Vanessa. The interviewer had left notes in the transcript that revealed not just what Barnaby had said, but also how he behaved. Telling the story of that jump, Barnaby's eyes had been wide open, fixed on the ceiling, as if he could, right at that very moment, see them jump from the plane.

Vanessa excitedly nudged Barnaby, poked a smile into him. They were jumping now, one after the other, the instructor pointing at them and shouting.

"Go!" Barnaby jumped without hesitation, Vanessa right behind him.

That moment of letting go. Barnaby's eyes were

closed, he felt a rush of excitement. And the same time a sense of serenity flooded him. Smiling, he opened his eyes and saw Vanessa right before him, descending at the exact same speed. She took his hand, pulled close and kissed him. Suddenly a grin spread across her face as she pulled his ripcord.

As if pulled by a taut rubber-band he was yanked up and an instant later, Vanessa's parachute was open, too.

Two parachutes floating gently, together, way up there.

~

Martha sat on the couch, staring at nothing, red-eyed, cried-out. She had used up the tissues but hadn't touched the pills. She had been wailing within the walls of her apartment. She didn't want attention, she couldn't face other people. And yet at some point she had wondered.

Weren't there neighbors?

Didn't anybody hear?

Didn't anybody care?

She was too close, too close to Barnaby Smith. Too close still, after all these months, to her son's death. You should stop, Martha. She couldn't, she couldn't stop.

Giving up on Barnaby Smith meant giving up on life.

If you give up, you die. Death is waiting.

She took the lacquered box, opened it, shook out two pills. The room, the room was spinning and everything blurred, the pictures on the walls, the world of Barnaby Smith, a blur, a hypnotizing blur.

She snapped back when the phone rang and rushed to pick it up. As she spoke, she slid the pills back in the box and closed it.

"Martha Lewis ... Yes?" She felt the ground open beneath her when she heard Charles' voice, when she understood what he was telling her. "Please no ..." she whispered as the phone slipped from her grip.

It was less than thirty minutes later when Martha rushed through the doors of the hospital. She looked exactly how she felt as she ran through the deserted hallway, a woman gone mad. Her hair unkempt, her face unwashed, her blood-shot eyes wide.

No time to clean up, no time to pretend.

She rushed to Barnaby's room, found the bed empty and an orderly in the bathroom cubicle, in the process of mopping up a smeared pool of blood. Martha stared at the blood, stared in complete shock. She heard the wind rushing in her ears, she saw her son falling to his death, landing with that unspectacular thud.

Blood. So much blood.

She felt herself losing balance, stumbling.

Two strong hands caught her just in time. She looked into the eyes of Charles.

"Come with me," he said.

She allowed him to guide her to his office where he placed her in one of the easy chairs. Through her shock, she noticed that he was disheveled – he wasn't wearing his bow tie. Who are you, she was tempted to ask. As if on cue, Charles took a bow tie from his desk and bound it within seconds to perfection. He set a cup of tea before her and sat down across from her.

"He called out around two," Charles began. "Said he needed to go to the bathroom. The guard undid the restraints. Somehow ... Barnaby managed to knock him unconscious."

"How did he ..." Charles shook his head in disbelief.

"The guard carried a pocket-knife with him."

"Can I see him?"

Barnaby lay on the infirmary bed, eyes closed, restrained, hooked up to IV drips and monitors, his wrists tightly bandaged. Bharad rose when Charles and Martha entered. Martha approached the bed slowly, acknowledged Bharad with a nod. He nodded back.

"He will live," Bharad said, his voice hard.

Martha couldn't blame him. He had to hate her, she hated herself. Her fault. All her fault. Tommy. Was Tommy her fault, too? Did she kill her son?

"I -," Martha began but Bharad cut her off.

"You were wrong."

Martha simply nodded. She looked down at the sleeping Barnaby. Tears welling up again but they didn't come. Her eyes burned as she stood there. Just stood there, helpless, useless.

Go kill yourself, Martha.

Go get it over with.

~

She couldn't remember what time she got there. She couldn't even remember how she got into the building. The building where they'd lived before. Martha, John and Thomas, the Lewis family. The happy home until Tommy had put an end to all of that.

She woke up on the roof of the building, shivering, sitting curled against the ledge. As she snuck out of the building, trying to avoid the super and old neighbors, she thought of that saying 'Dying is easy, living is hard'.

She tried to convince herself that something inside of her wanted to live, that hers was the harder choice, the braver choice.

But the louder voice in her head just said 'You're nothing but a coward, Martha Lewis.'

## NOTES FROM HIS DIARY

I had failed again. That was my first thought when I woke after the attempt. I couldn't feel my body and yet I knew that I was stitched up, bandaged and tied down.

I didn't feel entirely bad when I realized that the cocoon was back in full splendor. Nothing mattered once more. I was safe. Safe in the clouds of the unchanging skies. It was the next best thing to being dead.

It was only later that I thought about Bharad and Martha and what my suicide attempt had put them through. But even today, looking back, I believe my actions at the time where the only sensible option.

I'm selfish, more so than others, perhaps. But we're all selfish creatures. We do what we want, we do what we need - so that we can feel.

There is strength in that, there is happiness in that.

And there is certainty in that.

One life, my life, my choice.

The choice was death.

So many accounts of levitation are connected to religion in some form or other. And so of course I've asked myself … is there a god? There's certainly no evidence, but there's always the 'what if'.

What if there is a god? What if there is an afterlife? What if I get to see Vanessa and Aura again?

I didn't think about these things back then. I just wanted to settle back into my cocoon.

It was over.

Desperate Martha Lewis would leave me alone. Bharad would take care of me as he always had.

## GOOD NEWS OF SORTS

An inquiry followed Barnaby's suicide attempt and that meant Martha was asked to take a leave of absence until all questions were answered to the satisfaction of the board. She stayed in her apartment, shut out the world and waited. When the phone finally rang, she opened her eyes and looked around – the apartment was a mess.

"Yes," Martha spoke gruffly into the phone.

"Martha, it's Charles." She could hear the nervousness in his voice. "How are you?"

"What is it, Charles?"

"Well actually, I have good news," he said.

She realized that she was gripping the phone tightly and willed herself to relax her fingers. Good news. Whatever that meant.

"The inquiry is over," Charles continued. "You're back on duty as of tomorrow. That is, if you're ready."

"I am."

"Good, good," Charles said, chuckling. "Steward had planned a bit of a rebellion to take my place. Said my judgment had been clouded because of our, you know, history."

"Was it?" she asked, more sharply than intended.

"No, of course not. You are an excellent psycho-therapist, Martha. And the board backed my decisions. Needless to say, Steward wasn't pleased."

"How is Barnaby?"

"Recovering."

"It was too fast. I'll balance it differently next time. I

think I know how - "

"Martha," Charles interrupted. "There won't be a next time. The board's decision was unanimous. Barnaby is under Steward's care again." She stared at herself in the mirror, disheveled, worn, old. "You understand, don't you?"

"Yes." That's all Martha managed to say before hanging up.

She imagined Charles in his office, standing by the window, the dead phone still at his ear. She felt bad for him. But losing Barnaby felt worse. She couldn't put it into words. It wasn't just her need to help him. It wasn't just her desperate clinging to that one elusive bit of hope. It was more.

There was something more about Barnaby Smith.

~

Life at St. Joseph's was back to the way it had been during her first week there. Everything was, once more, structured, clean and orderly ... and medicated. Martha focused her energies on her patients, listening, suggesting, offering. It was obvious that the people in her care didn't just improve, they truly liked her.

Whether it was guilt or just trying to do as she had promised Charles, she stayed away from Barnaby and Bharad. Still, she noticed Steward watching her whenever she happened to be in the vicinity of Barnaby. And yes, sometimes it did happen.

She found herself drifting toward Barnaby and it would break her heart seeing him, sitting out there on the lawn again, staring up into the sky with empty eyes. Bharad, too, had clearly been given instructions to keep his distance from Dr. Martha Lewis. They hardly ever saw each other and when they did, Bharad didn't smile, turned around and walked away.

Is this it? Martha asked herself one afternoon, standing in her office by the window. She watched a lone bird in the sky. She wasn't getting better. That black hole in her stomach kept sucking her dry, dead. That hole. It wasn't closing, wasn't healing. Whatever she was doing, it wasn't working.

She gave a start when a knock rattled her door. Martha quickly took a seat, covered her pill box with a file and tried to look busy.

"Come in," she called.

To her surprise, it was Bharad. He approached her desk timidly, reached across and handed her a card.

"What is this?"

"My farewell party," Bharad said.

"… I'm invited?"

"Of course you are," he said, smiling.

Martha was stunned. She felt like jumping to her feet, bouncing around the desk and hugging the little man.

"Thank you," she said softly.

# I AM HERE

So much for promises. She felt better because she'd broken the promise to stay away. She felt better because of Barnaby and Bharad. Besides, she wasn't doing anything. She was just … there. She just happened to be in the cafeteria at lunch time. There was Barnaby, drooling, being fed by Bharad like a baby. Martha sat down next to Bharad and watched Barnaby's face.

"Barnaby," she said quietly.

Bharad just lightly shook his head.

"You know the dosage Dr. Steward is giving him."

"I know," Martha replied, her eyes still on her former patient. "Barnaby." He chewed, swallowed, slowly, slowly, opened his mouth again, waiting for the next spoon, all the time staring straight ahead.

"I am not giving up," Martha said softly.

As if in slow-motion, Barnaby's head turned, his eyes focusing on her.

"What are you doing?" Steward's voice. He had appeared out of nowhere and was suspiciously staring down at them.

"Oh hello, Dr. Steward," Martha said amiably.

"I must ask you to stay away from Barnaby Smith," Steward said importantly. "Your proximity may have an unsettling effect."

"I was just enjoying my break with a member of the staff," she replied as she stood. "It was nice seeing you, Bharad."

She gave Bharad a smile, Steward a nod and left without another glance back. Glowering, Steward's eyes stayed on her.

## NOTES FROM HIS DIARY

Life in death didn't return to normal. While, on the surface, everything seemed as it was supposed to be, I felt a change in the air. I was back in the care of Dr. Steward and yet Martha was around me when he wasn't looking.

And when she told me, that day in the cafeteria, that she wasn't giving up, she broke through to me. It was the strangest sensation and I believe that's when my cocoon cracked. I've been medicated for so many years, I know that to be impossible – those walls will not fall. And yet something happened that day. I felt the crack, I heard the crack – I was there and I felt the connection getting stronger.

I saw Martha's face, in the sky at first, through the clouds. But it became clearer and stronger and her eyes put another crack into the cocoon. I couldn't speak, I couldn't do anything at all when suddenly I wanted to tell her everything I had learned.

Why have human beings always looked to the skies, wanting to be up there, wanting to fly? Why do you think that is, Martha? I wanted to ask her about her dreams. We've all had them, dreams of flight, happiness in flight, freedom in flight. Those were not just dreams, I wanted to tell her. Human beings have always wanted to fly because we were meant to. It is within all of us, it is an activation of the mind. Why do we fly in our dreams? Because we remember it.

I wanted to tell her about the deceptions, the

tricksters and everything that made it so easy to dismiss every possibility of human flight. But there was myth, history, records, facts – stories from Egypt to China and from Russia to Europe. Stories witnessed and recorded by many. When Martha broke through that day something changed. There I was, drooling and Bharad gently wiping my beard. There I was, trying to tell, trying to share, trying to shout.

For the first time in years, there was hope.


## MERLIN & SMITH

Barnaby's file was on Steward's desk, but that didn't remove him from Martha's mind and, she figured, what she did in her spare time was nobody's business. She stood across the street from the pet shop she had read about in the files. It looked tiny, smaller even than the way she had imagined it. Stuck in between a manicure salon and a dry-cleaner, the pet shop seemed to struggle for air. There was no movement, no indication that the shop was even open other than the 'We're open' sign.

The shop window was cluttered with caged birds, hamsters and bunnies, crammed in between colorful assortments of accessories for cats and dogs. Martha smiled at the name across the top of the shop 'Merlin & Smith's Pet Shop'. She hurried across the street, jumped past a speeding cab and entered the shop. The bell above the door sounded as old-fashioned as the smell and feel of this place. Old. Good old.

She felt herself literally pulled toward the back of the store where she knew the bird cage room would be. She heard the birds before she saw them and then she stood and watched them hop and fly and sing and chatter and she could almost see the young Barnaby standing in their midst. She gave a start when she heard a voice.

"Can I help you?"

She knew that the cracked old voice with the French accent belonged to the owner, Maurice Merlin. She turned to see him walk toward her, wearing thick glasses. He must be in his eighties now, Martha thought.

"You must be Maurice Merlin."

He lightly bowed with a charming smile.

"The one and only. And you are?"

"Dr. Lewis, Martha Lewis. Barnaby Smith is my patient," she said and meant it. Regardless of where Barnaby's case was assigned, she felt responsible. It wasn't a lie – Barnaby Smith was her patient.

"Ah, Barnaby," Merlin said and sighed heavily. After a moment, the old man's Maurice Chevalier smile was back and he pointed to the bird room. "Come with me."

He opened the mesh wire door expertly, keeping an eye on every bird, talking to them to keep them in check as he ushered Martha in. He joined her and quickly closed the door again. Merlin began to replenish bird feed, added water, making chattering sounds as the birds hopped onto his shoulder, flew around him.

"Just talk to them," Merlin said without looking at Martha. "Don't be shy. They'll come say hello before you know it."

Awkward. Martha had never been a whistler, certainly never a chatterer. But Merlin ignored her, the birds stared at her and here she was, standing in the middle of the room, Barnaby's favorite place, feeling ludicrous.

Merlin winked at her, imitated a chattering budgie and motioned for her to do the same. At first the sounds wouldn't come but soon, to her surprise, her mouth began to produce what sounded like a form of 'budgie' to her.

She lost time. As Merlin went about the room, filling, cleaning, fixing – chattering all the time – she found herself swarmed by the birds. Afraid to move at first, she soon began walking around, stretching out her arms, making bridges and branches for the birds to jump and climb. Some sat on her head, others pecked at her fingers and hopped sideways along her arm until they nibbled on her earlobes. She felt feathers brushing her nose as the birds flew past her, around her, again and again. The old man began to speak.

"He just kept coming to the shop. Barnaby. Thirteen he was. Just kept coming. So I hired him. He was orphan. Had no one, you know."

"Yes, I know. ... do you have family?"

"Certainly. All my little friends here - and Barnaby, of course."

"I've never seen you at St. Joseph's," Martha said and instantly knew that she'd hit a sore spot in Merlin's heart. He turned away.

"I cannot bear it," he said and ushered her out. Blocking an adventurous canary from flying out, he skipped out behind Martha and closed the door. He looked at Martha and when he spoke, it sounded like an apology.

"I've always helped the boy. Whenever he jumped, when whatever happened. I was the best man, I was the godfather to beautiful little Aura. I even made him my partner – 'Merlin & Smith', you know. ... I cannot help him anymore. It's terrible."

There was more. Martha could see him remembering something. She stayed silent, gave him the time he needed. Finally, he pointed at the cage.

"One time, he must have been around fifteen, I saw him. I came from there, stood right here – and I saw Barnaby in there … He was flying, Dr. Lewis. Barnaby was in there, with his arms spread wide … and his feet did not touch the ground."

The old man stood there, arms spread wide. He saw the questions in Martha's eyes and dropped his arms.

"I know what you're thinking. Old man, crazy man. Probably a trick of the light. Look at his glasses. Maybe he wasn't even wearing them that night. And maybe he had a bit too much Cognac, too."

"You say you saw Barnaby levitate?" Martha asked.

Of course it was ludicrous. Of course it was impossible. So why even ask, Martha, why bother the old man, why not just leave him with his memories.

"Maybe I did drink too much," Maurice Merlin said. "Maybe Barnaby was just standing on his toes. Maybe … maybe I just want it to be true."

# THE FLYING FRIAR

It was late night and Martha had no intention of sleeping anytime soon. In her apartment, a new section to the Barnaby wall was forming. Martha was searching, printing, reading and pinning everything she could find on levitation.

Levitation was impossible. Simple physics, plain logic, basic common sense, levitation was impossible.

And yet Martha dug into everything she could find, looked for the obvious fakes, the magic tricks, the illusions as well as all the legends. There were stories upon stories, seemingly countless. People rising into the air, reported across centuries, continents, religions. Jesus walking on water, gurus floating above ground, prophets suspended in the air.

There were books and witness accounts.

Impossible, of course.

But Martha kept hearing the voice of Maurice Merlin.

"With his arms spread wide … and his feet did not touch the ground."

Even if she didn't believe flying was possible, and she didn't, she knew that Barnaby did. He believed it was possible.

And if he believed it, she needed to know about this, all of this. She learned about Indian sages, shamans, nuns and monks. She read stories that sounded fanciful and others that were reported to have been witnessed by hundreds of people.

Among those stories was the one of St. Joseph of Cupertino, a dim-witted man who became known across Europe as the Flying Friar. Not only that, he was seen flying by the Pope himself. He became so famous that the church eventually locked him away and kept him in complete isolation, afraid that he was becoming a cult figure.

More than one hundred years after the friar's death the Roman Catholic Church compiled his case, putting together more than a thousand pages detailing his life and his more than seventy recorded flights. The church arrived at the conclusion that all of those levitations, all of those witness accounts over the course of many years - and coming from men of stature and rank - were irrefutable proof. No mass hallucinations, no organized hoaxes – the simpleton monk had indeed levitated.

He was eventually canonized, proclaimed a saint and Martha had to read twice what she saw.

*'St. Joseph of Cupertino has been declared the patron saint of air travelers, aviators, astronauts, people with a mental handicap, test takers and poor students.'*

Air travelers, aviators and astronauts. Martha smiled at the idea that all the pilots zigzagging across the skies were under the protection of a $17^{th}$ century levitating Franciscan monk. Her eyes fixed on the second part, 'people with a mental handicap'.

Martha frowned. Couldn't be.

She grabbed her laptop and brought up the hospital website. Martha clicked the 'About us'. A photo of Chief Administrator Dr. Charles Richards, smiling brightly. She scanned the text next to him and there it was. She found what she had not expected to find … and what some part of her had hoped to find. She leaned back in her chair and read it out loud.

"St. Joseph's Hospital takes its name from St. Joseph of Cupertino."

# HAPPY BIRTHDAY, BARNABY

The following morning Martha arrived early at St. Joseph's. Another day, just another day, she told herself. But it felt different and she couldn't ignore it. There was something new about the building, the grounds, her sense – something … unprofessional. She knew it was foolish and she didn't fight it.

She was an intelligent woman, a scientist, looking for reason, for proof, always. Well, used to be.

Now here she was, reading up on flying monks, considering impossible scenarios, thinking about things like faith and belief … and destiny.

She locked the door of her Mercedes and looked across the park. Barnaby. He was walking slowly, a snail. A shell without a mind. Bharad followed Barnaby, as always two steps behind him, observing, alert. She knew he'd be there to catch Barnaby, always. To have a friend like that, Martha marveled.

She heard another car approach and moments later Charles stood next to her. He noticed her watching Barnaby but ignored it. Good man, Martha thought.

"Good morning, Martha."

"Hi Charles."

"… Looks like rain later today." Would Charles ever stop being awkward around her? Would she want that? She smiled at him and his face lit up.

"I didn't know that St. Joseph's was named after the patron saint of fliers," Martha said. She kept her eyes on his, intent on spotting his reaction, but he didn't seem to make a connection. And why would he? There is nothing there.

"Yes. Curious, isn't it?"

"Charles … do you think there is a plan?"

"A plan?" he said, frowning. "Oh, as in predestined, that sort of thing? Of course not. No. What you see is what you get is all there is. We are the plan, Martha, our choices and our actions. Well, gotta run. Catch you later," Charles said enthusiastically, leaving a pensive Martha behind.

What had she expected? He had just given her the answer she herself would have given before meeting Barnaby Smith.

~

Bharad solemnly entered the community room. He walked carefully, balancing a big cake, adorned with far too many burning candles. Martha followed, carrying plastic plates and spoons. Like a procession, they made their way toward Barnaby, who sat alone at a table across the room.

As Bharad began singing 'Happy Birthday' a few of the patients and members of staff looked up, most didn't. Martha felt uncomfortable, she'd never been a singer, but today she joined Bharad.

"Happy birthday to you, happy birthday to you, happy birthday dear Barnaby, happy birthday to you."

Between him, Martha and a few tone-deaf patients, a cacophony of sounds that only remotely resembled the song, reached Barnaby. Bharad put the cake on the table in front of Barnaby and sat opposite him. Martha stood at a distance.

"Happy birthday, Barnaby," Bharad said, smiling brightly.

All show, Martha knew. Barnaby kept looking through Bharad, no reaction.

"I will blow out the candles for you. Fifty-five, if you want to count them!"

An eager young patient helped Bharad blow them all out and for a moment there was thick smoke rising from the cake, Barnaby in a haze. He didn't move a muscle.

'This is the saddest birthday I have ever seen,' Martha thought and was impressed by how bravely Bharad continued with the show. He applauded and Martha and a few others joined in.

"All right, who wants cake?"

Martha handed him the plates and a dozen patients lined up for their slice. As Bharad handed out slice after slice, Barnaby moved. He slowly raised his hands, still looking at nothing, no emotion in his face. It was impossible to guess what he was going to do. Martha and Bharad stared at him, transfixed.

They watched as Barnaby's fingers slowly clawed into the cake. Bharad tried to pull the cake away but Barnaby's hands were buried in it. He pulled the cake toward him, off the table, landing half of it in his lap, the other half on the ground. Through all of this, there was still no movement in Barnaby's face.

Martha leaned in closer, trying to read something, anything, in Barnaby's eyes. Suddenly she saw it. A flicker, increasing, eyes widening. No doubt she was interpreting all the wrong things but she distinctly felt that Barnaby Smith was screaming for help.

She sat down next to him and took his cake-covered hand. His fingers locked around her hand and he gripped so hard it began to shake. Bharad nodded at her, glad for her help. Tears in his eyes, he proceeded to clean up the birthday mess.

As Barnaby gripped her hand, as Bharad scooped cake into a pail, Martha knew that she had to do something. Something entirely unprofessional. Something completely irresponsible. Something stupid. Something wrong.

Something right.

## NOTES FROM HIS DIARY

I have researched Daniel Dunglas Home as much as many others have – maybe more. He was, in the mid-19th century, one of the world's most famous mediums, well-known across Europe and the United States. He held countless séances, was entranced hundreds of times and levitated before many witnesses. He may have been a showman but I don't believe that to be the case. I believe that his mind connected differently and activated the greater potential of what we all hold within us. He flew and yet today we find it easier to shrug it all off. Do we shrug off the saints, the prophets?

I remember the day of my birthday ... the last of my birthdays inside St. Joseph's Hospital. It was the day when I reached her. Ever since she put a crack into my cocoon, I had tried to reach out to her, to give Martha a sign. If she could reach in, I could reach out. If she didn't give up, neither would I.

I had discovered hope and was clinging to it as I was clawing into that cake. A good cake, by the way. Bharad had made it himself, as he told me later. As I was bathing in that irrational pool of hope, I realized that it was no different from Martha's desperation. Hope and desperation are just two sides of the same coin. I wanted to spin it and I couldn't. I still couldn't speak. But I understood and I hoped and I believed that something could change. That something would change.

There was no doctor in her eyes that day, all pretense of detached professionalism gone. I had no idea what her plan was and neither did Martha. But I saw something forming. I saw a fire in her eyes and suddenly I knew that she would stop at nothing now. Looking back, I still marvel at what she and Bharad came up with. It was crazy then, it is crazy now. And I believe it was the only way.

# THE MIND IS EVERYTHING

It was dark when Martha drove the Mercedes out of St. Joseph's. She had waited in her office, her eyes on the street below, waited for Bharad to leave. She found him waiting for the bus around the corner from the hospital. He seemed even smaller, Martha thought, and older. He looked so sad, standing there, staring at his shoes. Martha stopped the car next to him and lowered the window.

"Dr. Lewis?"

"I'm going to save Barnaby," she said.

"What do you –"

"Will you help me?" Martha asked. This was mad and she knew it.

"I don't understand – "

"Will you help me save Barnaby?" she asked urgently. "Yes or no?" Confused, Bharad frowned at her, then nodded with conviction. "Get in."

Still frowning, Bharad got in. And the frowning continued when, thirty minutes later, he stood in front of the 'Barnaby wall' in Martha's apartment. He studied every document, every image, stepped back, stepped in, engrossed, fascinated, concerned. Martha didn't say a word. She just stood by the kitchen counter and waited for his reaction. He finally turned to look at her.

"So you … want us to kidnap Barnaby? I am sorry, but - this is crazy."

"Illegal, yes. Crazy, no," Martha said, trying to make herself believe it.

"Out here he will kill himself."

"Out here we can give him hope," Martha argued. "In there he will stay dead."

Bharad pointed at the pictures of levitations, the prophets, the saints, the gurus.

"But those are all just stories."

"Stories representing his belief. That man can fly," Martha said.

"But man cannot fly!"

"Bharad," she said, staring at him, "you agreed to help me save Barnaby."

Bharad looked at the pictures on the wall again. Martha was surprised when he suddenly took out his phone.

He motioned for patience as he made a call, spoke a few words in Hindi before turning to Martha again.

"We must go to Queens."

~

Bharad directed her to Jackson Heights, a Queens neighborhood also called 'Little India'. Martha parked the car and followed Bharad through a street where every shop seemed to sell Indian clothes, jewelry and Bollywood DVDs. At the corner building, Bharad rang a bell three times and moments later a shrieking buzzer allowed them entry.

"You're still not telling me what we're doing here?" Martha asked.

Bharad, climbing the narrow stairs, looked back and shook his head. Wheezing, he continued up to the third floor and knocked on a door.

"Enter," a voice called from within. Bharad opened the door and signaled for Martha to enter first. The flat was a curious sight. The room seemed like a small Indian temple, with ornaments, statues and candles everywhere.

The person in the middle of the room was even more curious. In the glow of the candle light, a long-haired and long-bearded guru was levitating. This is impossible, Martha thought, a trick. It must be a trick. The man was clearly sitting in the air, three feet off the ground. He wore a wide robe and his left hand was lightly holding a staff that reached the floor. Martha turned to look at Bharad.

"Enough?" the guru said.

"Sure, thank you, Sachin. Dr. Lewis. This is my cousin Sachin."

Martha nodded a hello, realizing that she felt shy, as if afraid the man would crash to the floor if she spoke.

"Would you mind giving me a hand?" the guru asked. Bharad stepped next to him and helped him off a metal contraption that had been hidden underneath the robe. Martha raised her eyebrows, so that's how it was done. Two steel plates attached ingeniously to both ends of the staff that merely looked like a simple wooden stick. All of it was made of steel, the plate at the bottom hidden underneath the rugs, the plate at the top the seat for the guru, expertly hidden underneath the robe.

"That's how Sachin makes a living," Bharad explained. "You may have seen him on Times Square? He's quite an attraction."

"It's inventive," Martha said. Sachin, looking like a picture-book guru, stood next to them and listened with polite interest.

"And it is fake," Bharad said. "That's why I brought you to see this. None of these stories are real. How should any of this help Barnaby?"

"Ah, cousin," Sachin suddenly intoned, "All that we are is the result of what we have thought. The mind is everything. What we think we become." Bharad gave Sachin an annoyed glance and Sachin shrugged. "It was the only 'Buddha' I could think of just now. Anybody want a beer?"

When nobody said anything, Sachin shrugged and shuffled off.

"There is no other way," Martha said fervently. The more the idea was percolating in her mind, the more it made sense to her. "A life for Barnaby, Bharad, a life. Remember? A real life. Nothing at St. Joseph's will ever give him that."

Bharad looked at the floor as if ashamed.

"... I know about your son, Dr. Lewis," he finally said. "Dr. Steward told me. Is that why you are doing this?"

Martha forced herself to keep looking at him, forced herself to keep her calm – it didn't work. She felt herself shake, felt painful tears burning in her eyes.

"Yes. No. My son. My Tommy. I've been thinking about joining him since the moment he jumped off that roof. I ... I miss him so much ... but it's not that. It's not me. Not just me. You have to believe me."

Bharad awkwardly approached and tried to give her a hug. Martha pulled away and grabbed his shoulders.

"Please. Bharad. Please. We can save him."

"... I will make a very bad criminal," Bharad finally said and shyly smiled. Martha impulsively hugged him with all her might.

Sachin, now wearing regular clothes, came back with three beers in hand. When he saw the woman hugging his cousin, he silently retreated into the kitchen again. Whatever was going on there, he didn't want to know.

# SIGN OF THE EAGLE

Charles Richards wasn't as puzzled as he pretended to be. Two things made him behave the way he did. For one, he liked Martha, for another, he couldn't say the same thing about his esteemed colleague Dr. Henry Steward who was currently seated across from him, still and stern. Charles kept his puzzled look in place.

"I'm afraid I don't understand what you're telling me."

"There is something going on, that's what I'm telling you," Steward snapped.

"Because ...," Charles prompted.

"Because," Steward repeated, clearly exasperated now, "despite the fact that Barnaby Smith is clearly assigned to my care, she is spending an inordinate amount of time in his company - and in the company of Barnaby's nurse."

"But you just said that she doesn't interfere with your work. I really don't see -"

"There is something going on! Look out the window. Go ahead." Steward jumped to his feet and to the window, daring Charles to follow.

When Charles followed Steward's furiously pointing finger, he found he didn't have to pretend to be puzzled any longer. He was. Down there, on the grass, three people were seated next to one another. Barnaby in the middle, Martha to his left and Bharad to his right. They all sat there with their backs to the building, looking up into the sky.

"Tell me that looks like a normal doctor patient relationship to you." He was right, of course he was right. Charles did his best to hide his concern. He wasn't about to give Steward the satisfaction.

"But she's not his doctor," he simply replied.

"That's exactly what she says," Steward shot back. "She says she's just spending her breaks on the grounds." Steward bit his lip before he continued. "Look, I'm sorry about what happened with the board. Yes, I'd love your position but this isn't about me now. Dr. Richards, please. Tell me that doesn't look strange to you."

"All right," Charles finally said. "I'll talk to her." Steward nodded curt thanks and charged off. Charles turned back to the window, wondering, worried.

~

What am I doing? Martha looked to Barnaby and Bharad, sitting next to her in the grass. This was careless. She should be anywhere but here, with them. This would draw attention, this would make Steward even more suspicious. But it felt right. It felt like this, right here, right now, was exactly the place where she needed to be.

Barnaby's eyes were fixed on the sky as usual. He was breathing calmly, deeply. There was nothing to see, just sky, just clouds. Martha knew that, with all of his medication, Barnaby's mind was numbed, a wide and empty space.

"The day you arrived here," Bharad said, "we saw a bird way up there. A big bird – I believe it was an eagle."

"I didn't think there were eagles around here," Martha replied.

"There aren't," Bharad said, his face raised to the sky

like Barnaby. "And still that bird was there. It may have been a sign, Martha, an omen."

"An omen? Hardly."

"You don't believe in such things."

Martha didn't answer. Fate. Destiny. New considerations she hadn't contemplated before. Certainly hadn't believed before. But now she considered. Why not add 'omen' to her growing list of 'what ifs'.

"You know," Bharad continued, "I thought that eagle was here for Barnaby ... Maybe I was wrong. Maybe it was here for you."

Martha frowned and snuck a glance across at Bharad. His eyes continued to be fixed on the sky, a smile on his face. She looked at Barnaby. Unchanged. She gently wiped a spit bubble from the corner of his mouth, then she, too, focused on the sky again.

~

Bharad had asked her again and again. What was the plan? Getting Barnaby out of St. Joseph's was difficult enough – but after that? Martha had stalled him. Not because she didn't have a plan but because she needed to come to grips with it herself. She tried to convince herself that it was the only thing that would give Barnaby a chance. For her plan to work, he needed to disappear.

She watched Bharad, sitting on her couch, reading a book entitled "The History of Human Levitation". The coffee table was littered with leftover food and drink. Bharad's forehead was creased with worry lines, his lips silently mouthing the words as he read them. When he finally closed the book, he didn't look up and Martha forced herself to be patient. Wait. Give him a chance to think it through.

"That is your plan?" he asked in disbelief.

"Yes."

"This is your whole plan?"

"Yes," she repeated forcefully. "It is a quest. It will give him strength. It will give him time to discover the will to live."

"And how are we supposed to get there?"

"I don't know," she said, watching him intently. He wasn't dismissing the idea. He was thinking about it. Bharad was blankly staring at the wall.

"We will need money," he suddenly said.

"I have money. What are you thinking about? Do you have an idea?"

"No. We'll have to get Barnaby secretly out of the

country."

"You do have an idea, don't you?"

"I have to call a cousin," Bharad said.

"Sachin?"

"I have many cousins."

## NOTES FROM HIS DIARY

They didn't change my medication and they didn't tell me anything about their plans. It wouldn't have registered anyway. I felt everything, as always. But the connections in my mind were mostly wrong and, where they were right, they were padded in soothing layers of chemical down once more.

In those days we became conspirators. Martha spent more time with us, in brazen disregard of Dr. Steward. I remember smiling a lot, mostly on the inside. A vague smirk would occasionally slide across my lips and Martha would catch it and smile back. Just a twitch, facial muscles acting independently. And maybe it was a first attempt of breaking free. Maybe it was her desperate courage that give me strength.

With therapy firmly back in the hands of Dr. Steward, she stopped being the psychiatrist. She was just there. I would sit and stare into the clouds as always – and listen to her voice, to her conversation with Bharad. I felt a closeness, the beginning of friendship, whispered words and casual laughter. I felt a warmth that radiated from the two people near me.

When we sat in the grass, the three of us, I felt good. I felt calm. Good calm, clear calm.

I began to think that maybe this was it. Maybe I was finally getting there, to that clarity of mind where my body would leave the ground.

For thousands of years, people had taken flight in moments of ecstasy, in moments of crisis, in moments of calm. Some levitated in their sleep, many in a state of meditation. In addition, there were the mediums, like Daniel Dunglas Home, people who would levitate in a trance.

I wanted more.

I have always wanted more. I don't want meditation, I don't want trance.

I will be wide awake when I fly.

The mind is everything.

# A NEW BEGINNING

It was Bharad's final day. After more than three decades at St. Joseph's, retirement would be his new best friend. Everyone had assembled in the community room under a big farewell banner that had been hand-painted by patients. It read, in all available colors:

'GoodBie, ALL tHeBest!
Good luck. WewiLl Miss YoU!!!'

Bharad was clearly ill at ease but put on a brave face. It was well known that he didn't want to leave, that he didn't have a life outside of St. Joseph's, that leaving Barnaby behind was tantamount to betraying a best friend. But he smiled as nurses and patients alike came to hug him. He accepted their gifts, their heartfelt comments, their pats on the back.

Martha glanced over to Barnaby who sat motionless in a chair, staring straight ahead. Martha lightly nodded to herself and realized at that moment that she was being watched.

She caught Charles looking at her. He quickly switched from a frown to a smile. Martha smiled back.

Under different circumstances … Charles called for attention.

"Everybody, please!" He took a paper cup, filled with warm white wine, and raised it in Bharad's direction. "Dear Bharad. You have been at St. Joseph's longer than anyone else – it has been thirty-six years!" The number was followed by a round of rousing applause and cheers. Charles smiled and asked for silence once more. "I've looked at the old files – and I've not found one single complaint. Not one. It seems you have always been as I've come to know you – an invariably caring and utterly reliable nurse ... and a first-rate human being. We will all miss you very much!"

They all crowded around Bharad, toasting paper cups one and all. Bharad laughed and cried and shook many hands. When he looked her way, Martha gave him a light nod and walked away.

As she left the room, she had to walk past Steward who gave her a thin smile.

For the past days he had been relentless in keeping an eye on her and Bharad. But you can't watch us both, Martha thought and smiled back at him as she passed.

~

The final duty on his final day. Bharad was in Barnaby's room and tucked him in the way he had done for twenty-three years. He removed the knitted cap, put it on the shelf, straightened Barnaby's hair and caressed his cheek.

"Tomorrow will be a new beginning," Bharad whispered.

"In what way?" Dr. Steward's voice demanded. Startled, Bharad turned to see Steward standing at the open door.

"My retirement, Dr. Steward. A new beginning tomorrow." Steward's eyes narrowed as he took a step toward Bharad.

"What are you planning?"

"I don't really know yet," Bharad said innocently. "Maybe visit my daughters. I would also like to see something of -"

"I have my eyes on you."

"What are you -" Bharad began but Steward cut him off, pointing a finger at him.

"If I catch you doing anything at all, I will revoke your visiting privileges. Do you understand? You will never see Barnaby again."

Head hanging low, Bharad nodded. With a final look at Barnaby, he left the room. Steward stared at Barnaby for another moment as if expecting him to rise. When nothing happened, he closed the door.

~

It wouldn't be easy, but she couldn't leave without saying good-bye. Martha took a deep breath before opening the door to Charles' office. He was there, bent over a file, looking up and smiling at the sight of her.

"Martha, everything okay?" She smiled and walked to him. Charles frowned.

"I just wanted to thank you, Charles."

"What have I done?"

"You have given me a chance." He rose awkwardly and smiled.

"It was my pleasure." Before he could say or do anything else, Martha hugged him – and let go again before he had a chance to hug her back. She turned and walked to the door.

"You are a good man, Charles."

"I'll see you tomorrow then," Charles said, trying to hide his confusion. Martha smiled at him. A smile that said 'I will miss you, Charles.'

~

Bharad closed his emptied locker. There was a man sitting on the bench behind Bharad, tied up, gagged, dressed in nothing but his underwear.

"I'm sorry," Bharad said.

The man simply nodded as if to say 'Don't worry about it'. Bharad picked up the man's clothes and stuffed them into a duffel bag.

"I'll have these washed and returned to you. But it may take a while."

Another understanding nod.

Everything fell into place exactly as Martha had planned. They were in the right places at the right time, when eyes were turned, when cameras looked the other way. No sign of trouble, no sign of Dr. Steward. The guards barely looked up when Bharad and Barnaby, dressed in a nurse's uniform, walked past. Doors were buzzed open without question or comment and Bharad forced himself to walk as leisurely as possible. Two blocks away from the hospital Martha was waiting with her car.

When she saw them approach, she got out, gave Bharad a hurried smile.

"How did it go?"

"We just walked out," Bharad said, shaking head at the smooth escape. "It was, it felt, as if they wanted us to leave."

"Steward won't be happy," Martha said with a smile.

She looked up at Barnaby. His face was blank, no recognition, no expression. He looked at Martha but didn't seem to see her. Martha tried an encouraging smile before she and Bharad huddled him into the backseat of the car.

And with that ... they disappeared into the night.

# CHAPTER TWO

# THE JOURNEY TO NEPAL

# NOTES FROM HIS DIARY

I'm trying to recall what happened after our escape. I noticed right away that there were no more pills … and that meant hurtling down a maelstrom of madness. That I guess is the literary way of putting it. What really happened was a nightmare of hallucinations, of clawing up the walls, of feverish silent screaming and drowning in boiling sweat. It wasn't pretty.

I have vague memories of a motel and a detailed image of a lamp shade with a stain in the shape of Italy. There were glimpses of Bharad and Martha and sometimes they looked like themselves and sometimes they were gargoyles coming to tear me apart. They cleaned me and fed me and cleaned me again.

I remember food that looked different and smelled different and tasted different from everything I had become accustomed to. We were all there in a room with red walls and soft beds and noises of people and cars just outside the door.

When I asked Martha about that time, those first days away from St. Joseph's, she didn't tell me much. But just looking at her face, and at Bharad shaking his head with an uneasy smile, I knew that it had been more than difficult. Climbing into those vague memories I see flashes of me trying to run away. I see them catching me, half naked, on the road. I see their desperation and their smiles and I see how they cling to a hope that has no right being there.

In flashes, I remember the pain and the urge to hit Bharad, to make his smile go away. My fists opening and closing and everything inside of me screaming for the white walls of St. Joseph's, and the grass and the clouds and the unchanging skies.

I remember cars, different cars. We moved more than once and after a while there was the smell of water, salt water, and a seagull screaming.

They half-carried me onto a big ship and there were dark faces looking at me. Martha was there and Bharad was there and they talked with soft, soothing voices, holding me, helping me, pushing me. I tried to tell them, I tried to explain that I needed to go home, home to St. Joseph's but they wouldn't listen and I wouldn't speak.

And I screamed and didn't make a sound.

A thousand hammers pounding away at my intestines and my heart and my chest and my brain.

Those days won't ever come back and it's best that way. Some things are not worth remembering.

I finally found myself in a room that wasn't mine and the porthole window suggested that we were on a ship. They were there, my friends, my enemies, my rescuers, my torturers, they were there when I found my voice and screamed. I continued until my throat felt as if it had been doused with acid.

In the end, what I remember most is Bharad's smile and I closed my eyes.

## GOOD-BYE AMERICA

They were inside Barnaby's cabin when he woke again. He looked around in confusion, not recognizing anything. Martha understood the danger but it was done, there was no turning back now.

She had torn Barnaby from the surroundings he had known to be his home for close to a quarter century.

And for what? A crazy idea that had more to do with her than it did with him?

No. No, Martha.

This is right. For him.

For both of you.

It was seven days since the kidnapping. They had

hidden away in a motel, paid cash, stayed indoors. Martha had ordered Barnaby off medication right away. Late last night they had made their way to the Red Hook container terminal. Now Bharad sat by the side of the bed, smiling, caressing Barnaby's cheek. Barnaby closed his eyes again, a hint of a tired smile on his lips.

A red-faced and clearly ill-tempered Indian entered the cabin. He wore a starched captain's uniform that stretched tightly across his round frame. The captain removed his hat and wiped the sweat from his forehead.

"Dr. Lewis," Bharad said, "this is my cousin Amit."

"Welcome on The Pride of India," the captain said curtly. "I've watched the news. The police is looking for this man."

"Cousin. I can assure you that we are only trying to help him."

"That is entirely your own business, not mine. I expect to be in Mumbai twenty-two days from now and then, as now, I will have never met you."

"Are there other passengers on board?" Martha asked.

"No passengers. Cargo and crew only."

"Thank you for your help," Martha said.

"My pleasure," he replied coldly and left. Martha

turned to Bharad.

"Can we trust him?"

"Worst of all of my cousins," Bharad said with a shrug. "But he is greedy and your money buys us his silence and that of his men."

Twenty-two days, Martha thought. Twenty-two days in the confines of the ship. Twenty-two days to hope, to live, to die. She looked at the sleeping Barnaby. A case, a man, unlike any she had ever met. No frame of reference. Anything could happen. Would happen.

Bharad had made himself comfortable in the chair next to Barnaby's bed.

His eyes were closed. He looked weak but content.

He was going home.

~

Martha stood on deck in a canyon between the countless containers that were stacked like Lego bricks. All she saw was a slice of the Atlantic and a slice of the sky. Seagulls up there, calling to each other.

It was only the second day on the ship.

She knew it would happen. Soon.

All she could do was wait.

The experience so far was the opposite of what she had expected. She'd had images of being stowaways, hidden away in dark holes, fed with old bread and stale water. Instead the captain, a lot more relaxed now that they were at sea, had already invited her for dinner. She had also met the crew at the canteen. Nice people from first to last, a dozen different nationalities with varying degrees of weathered faces.

When she went back to the cabin, she found Barnaby awake, Bharad next to him, shooting her a worried glance. He was in the process of cleaning and dressing Barnaby's forehead.

"What happened?" Martha asked.

"I was in the bathroom," Bharad said as he pointed at a bloody spot on the inside of the door. "I heard banging. When I came out I saw that Barnaby was standing at the door, banging his head against it, again and again."

She stepped closer and saw the clarity in Barnaby's eyes, saw him looking at her, really looking at her.

"We should give him something. To calm him down," Bharad said. Martha didn't reply, her eyes still fixed on Barnaby. "Dr. Lewis, please."

"No," she replied.

She couldn't read Barnaby. He looked worn and weak

but there was something more. Something darker.

"Do you know where you are, Barnaby?" she asked. He looked around, took in the cabin, the porthole window.

"Ship."

"Yes," Martha said. "We are on our way to India."

"Why?" he whispered and Martha could see that all energy had left him, his body weak, the violent incident with the door taking its toll. Bharad put a final bandage on Barnaby's brow, then took the bloody towels to the bathroom. Martha sat down next to Barnaby as his eyelids fluttered.

"You are going to fly, Barnaby." He frowned at her as his eyes closed. Just before falling into sleep, he spoke once more.

"Flying ... is impossible."

# FIVE DEAD ROBBERS

They whispered, standing by the door. Barnaby was deep asleep while Bharad wiped the blood stains from the door.

"It takes time," Martha said. She could see that Bharad was questioning everything. She couldn't blame him – and she couldn't help him. Only time would tell.

"But what if Barnaby just doesn't want to live anymore?" Bharad asked. "What if he does it again until he succeeds?" She knew these doubts, they were her own.

"Stay with him. We take turns," she said abruptly and left.

The following days were a constant hell of blood and tears, screams and vomit. Martha and Bharad took turns, didn't leave Barnaby from their sight for even a moment. They watched him, washed him, fed him as he suffered through every violent withdrawal stage. It came in bursts. One morning Martha could speak to him, that same afternoon he'd be screaming at her. One moment Barnaby might smile at Bharad, the next he'd be spitting food in his face. Martha and Bharad forced each other to eat and sleep but despite it all they looked more and more like the weakened Barnaby.

Today is a special day, Martha told herself. She had no way of knowing, but the hope was there. The last two days Barnaby had markedly improved. Now she sat at a small table in the ship's shabby canteen. She had showered and wore a fresh blouse, three plates of steaming stew on the table before her.

She looked up and smiled when the door opened. Bharad and Barnaby entered, both of them looking as if they'd cleaned up for a special occasion. Martha watched Barnaby closely as they joined her at the table. His movements were still slow, his hands shaking just slightly – but his eyes were crystal clear now.

"Enjoy," she simply said, took her spoon and began to eat. Bharad and Barnaby looked at each other and followed suit. Martha caught Bharad glancing sideways at Barnaby, checking on him.

He was eating. As if it were the most normal thing in the world. Just a man, sitting at a table with friends, eating. Martha and Bharad secretly smiled at each other.

"How long, since ..." Barnaby said.

"Eleven days. We've left New York eleven days ago," Martha replied. "How do you feel, Barnaby?"

"Sea-sick," he simply said and Martha smiled.

"How do you feel without your medication,

Barnaby?"

"Better," he said evenly.

Martha looked from him to Bharad and Bharad nodded. It was time to tell Barnaby.

"Good. Now let me tell you a story," Martha began.

~

The Boudhanath temple in Nepal's Kathmandu seemed to glow. The rays of the afternoon sun struck the golden sphere above the vast mound of the temple. From the highest top, ropes filled with colorful prayer flags stretched in every direction. It was a day of peace for most, a day of deadly horror for five careless men.

A severe-looking old monk left the temple and as he went, people seemed to shrink away from him. He was known, he was whispered about, he was left alone. There were stories about him. Dark stories. The monk didn't acknowledge anyone. He didn't smile, he didn't glare, he simply continued on his path as if unaware of the world around him.

As the monk made his way through markets and side streets and deserted back alleys, eyes followed him. An old woman, her spices spread on the ground before her, watched the monk pass by. She looked to the vendors around her – they had seen what she had seen. It had been he, the one only whispered about. It was something she'd be able to tell the family tonight. They wouldn't believe her, of course. But it didn't matter. She had really seen the monk – and she had no idea that her story was about to become legendary.

Five young men hurried after the monk. They were thieves, the old woman knew. One a nephew of a friend of hers. A life gone wrong but, until today, she had never considered it to be her concern. They were going to rob the monk! The old woman picked up her courage and shouted at those around her. They had all seen. They had to do something. Reluctantly, a few of the vendors took sticks in hand and followed the woman.

When they cautiously stepped around the corner, they saw something they would never forget. And something they would tell their friends and relatives until their dying day. Walking into a dead-end street, with no way out and a massive wall at the end, they found the five young men, struck dead. The monk, however, was gone. Horrified, the spectators gaped and shouted and remembered every story about the monk they'd ever heard before. It was all true.

He had killed those men with his magic.

And then he had flown away.

~

Barnaby, Martha and Bharad were on deck in between the containers. A strong wind blew salty air into their faces. Barnaby was leaning against one of the containers, eyes closed, taking slow, deep breaths.

"They don't know his name," Martha said when she had finished her story. "Everything about him is a mystery."

"I have never heard of this monk," Barnaby said as he opened his eyes.

"You couldn't have. I know you've done a lot of research, Barnaby. But the first story about this monk surfaced long after you arrived at St. Joseph's. Nine years ago, a tourist wrote a blog post about it."

"Blog," Barnaby said. "The internet, right?"

"You have a lot of catching up to do," Martha said, smiling at him. He lightly shook his head. No way of telling what he was thinking about but it made Martha frown and she saw that Bharad was worried, too.

"Listen to me, Barnaby. The most recent stories

appeared on the web, the internet, just months ago. This monk is alive. He is real. And we are going to find him."

She had poured every bit of conviction into her little speech and now all she could do was wait. Take the hook, Barnaby, take the hook.

"All right," he finally said, his voice even.

Too even? No excitement and a bare minimum of interest. Was that all she could hope for? Barnaby had already turned and walked away. Bharad gave her a shrug and hurried after Barnaby.


## NOTES FROM HIS DIARY

I had been around psychiatrists long enough. Did Martha believe in this elusive monk? Of course not. Did Bharad? I don't think so. It was supposed to be about the journey, not the goal. But what they didn't understand was that I didn't need a monk to fly. I just needed to try again. Until it worked. I could do that anywhere, anytime. At least that was what I believed at the time.

That day was my darkest moment. Going through the various stages of withdrawal was nothing compared to this. I had searched and learned and tried and jumped and failed my whole life. Even when I lay crushed and broken in a pool of my own blood I had never despaired, I had never gave up. Even at St. Joseph's, I had never known this agony. That day, when they told me about the monk, my mind cleared. For the first time since the moment of their death, every cloud was lifted from my memories.

I wasn't prepared for it. Even now I struggle, even now I try to push it all away. I wish I didn't see their faces. Moments before I killed them … moments after I killed them. For twenty-three years that pain had been hidden from me and now the anguish flooded my mind like a water bursting from a breaking dam. Once again I saw that day in every detail, I saw the car, the storks … everything there with perfect clarity. My wonderful Vanessa. And Aura, sweet Aura. And I realized that, remembering all of that, I would never be able to fly. How could I?

Everything that I had ever wanted was available to me now. I was free of the walls and free of the unchanging skies. I was in the company of two brave people who had risked everything for me. They had given up everything, for me. The wind. I could feel it on my skin like a gentle invite and the sky was calling to me.

It was all there … after so many years, it was all there.

And in all of that potential I knew that I wasn't free. I would never be free. All of my memories. Too much love, too much pain … too much weight. In that darkest moment, I knew that my freedom was an illusion. My hope was a fantasy.

## THE CAR WON'T FLY

She stood by the door as Bharad was about to put the restraints on Barnaby's wrists as they had done every night. Barnaby, lying in bed, looked to her.

"There is no need," he said.

Bharad frowned and turned to Martha, his eyes clearly signaling that the restraints had to stay on.

"Is flying possible, Barnaby?" Martha asked.

"Yes," he said without hesitation. With this she nodded and Bharad put the restraints aside. He tucked Barnaby in as he'd always done and Barnaby let it happen. "But you don't believe that," Barnaby said into the silence.

"I've read so much over the past weeks," Martha began. "I don't know. But I know that I want to believe. What if, Barnaby, what if."

Barnaby kept his eyes on her for a long moment and she had the distinct feeling that he was trying to assess her. He finally closed his eyes.

"Good night, Barnaby," she said.

His eyes remained closed. Maybe he was already asleep. Martha watched as Bharad, like some nesting creature, busied himself, piling blankets into the chair in the corner and finding the most comfortable position.

He gave Martha a nod and a smile and she quietly closed the door.

~

Little later she stood at the railing of the ship, alone in the night. The cold breeze of the Atlantic gnawing at her neck.

She didn't trust Barnaby. Couldn't. She had trusted her son. Had never even suspected her son. Now suspicion was a constant companion. The specter of death everywhere. And yet she tried, she had to try. If she could ever hope to gain his trust, she had to give it.

The stars were out in force and the moon shone a pale light. She noticed the captain strolling in her direction, his white uniform shimmering from afar. He acknowledged her silently as he stepped next to her.

"There is nothing more beautiful than a clear night on the open sea," he said.

She simply gave him a light smile, hoping he would leave again.

"If anything happens with that man," the captain continued, "No one will ever know. You were never on my ship."

"Nothing will happen, Captain."

"He is crazy."

"... It is a nice night," Martha said and he looked at her profile.

"Maybe you are crazy, too."

~

Crazy. Defining crazy wasn't that clear anymore. The lines blurred more and more as Martha walked down to her cabin. Crazy. Moments in time that change us forever.

What had it been for Barnaby? He had always been peculiar but somehow, despite his lasting obsession with flight, he had had a place in life. He had been a husband, a father, a co-owner of a pet shop. It was the accident that put him in St. Joseph's, that ended life not just for his wife and child, but for Barnaby, too. As Martha washed her face and brushed her teeth, she recalled the transcript. Barnaby's words.

He had talked about a beat-up blue Ford Escort and how he and Vanessa had hand-painted white clouds all over it. He had recalled the day they went for a drive, little Aura in the back next to a picnic basket.

"The car won't fly, Barnaby," Vanessa said with a grin. He smiled at her, slowing down just a little. In the field behind Vanessa, he spotted four storks, flying low in perfect parallel with the car. Barnaby was mesmerized and glanced back at his daughter.

"Look over there! Look, Aura – do you see the storks?" Barnaby was caught in the glow of the little girl's face. She shrieked with joy and, for that one brief moment, they felt as if they were flying with the storks … until Vanessa's scream.

"Barnaby! Watch -"

He had no recollection of the crash. He just remembered the moment before, the sight of an old tractor coming onto the road, off a dirt track. And Barnaby remembered the moments after, the face of the shocked farmer. And the blood, all that blood, where

Vanessa and Aura's smiling faces had been.

When Martha sank into her worn mattress and pulled the blanket to her chin, her final thought was the hope that Barnaby wouldn't remember everything.

## ARMS SPREAD WIDE

Barnaby opened his eyes. The first light of day shining through the porthole. Tilting his head, Barnaby looked to Bharad who was curled into the chair, a dozen blankets around and over him. Without making a sound, Barnaby left the room.

A clear and biting early morning greeted him on deck. He was alone with mountains of containers, endless sea and a wide open sky. The horizon was coming into focus, the sun would soon rise. Barnaby climbed onto the railing, swung his legs across and stood on the outside of it as the morning light increased. He rose to his full height, spread his arms, still leaning back against the rails.

The moment had come. Barnaby lightly pushed off and let himself fall forward, down toward the waves rushing past far below. He veered just before the splash and flew forward with the speed of the fall, just inches above sea level. He smiled as the sun rose, flooding him with warmth, forcing him to squint. Barnaby changed direction again and flew back to the ship, along and around its hull and up and into the container canyons.

Bliss. The only thing that mattered, as he hurled himself playfully through the narrow lanes between the ship's cargo, was the sky and the wind.

Flight.

Barnaby opened his eyes and recalled the dream. The sense of flight still strong within him, so strong it physically hurt as if an army of hammers were pounding against the inside of his rib cage. It was dawn. Bharad lay curled in the chair among the blankets. Barnaby slowly, cautiously, rose from his bunk. A creak of the mattress, Bharad didn't stir. Barnaby slowly pushed the chair with Bharad, blankets and all, away from the door.

Barefoot, he slipped from the room.

~

A glimmer of hope. Martha stepped out of the shower, wiped the mirror and looked at herself. She tried a smile and it came and it felt real. Toweling her hair, she thought about the journey up to this moment. They had succeeded in secretly moving Barnaby out of the country. They actually were on the way to find an elusive monk somewhere in the Himalayas. A story that was no doubt as real as the legend of Bigfoot and Yeti. She didn't care. Barnaby had stepped out of the thick fog he'd been living in for so many years. He was awake and he had listened. Yes, Martha said to herself, a glimmer of hope is justified.

Minutes later she strolled from hers to Barnaby's cabin and knocked.

"Rise and shine! Mind if I come in?"

Inside, something crashed and she heard Bharad mumble in Hindi. She was already reaching for the door when Bharad tore it open. She took in the room. Bharad's chair lay sideways on the floor, Barnaby's bed was empty.

"Where is he?"

"I don't know, I just -" Bharad stuttered, wide-eyed.

"You were supposed to watch him!" Martha screamed at him, both panic and fury. She turned and ran, to the stairs, up the stairs. Barnaby, no. She heard Bharad follow behind her.

"I'm sorry, Dr. Lewis!" Angrily, she looked down the stairs and saw him, hands at his chest, cringing with pain. She hurried back down.

"Bharad, are you all right?"

"Fine," he said, breathing heavily. "I'm fine, go find Barnaby!" He pushed her away, up the stairs. She ran, two, three steps at a time. At the next landing, she glanced back and saw, to her relief, that Bharad was following, grim and fast.

They split as soon as they were on deck. None of the crew members were in sight, the ship seemed empty. A ghost ship. It's just you and Bharad … and Barnaby. Where are you? She heard Bharad calling his name and it echoed from container to container.

"Barnaby!" she yelled at the top of her lungs. She crisscrossed the container lanes, always looking in every direction, always shouting his name. Her feet had already carried her past another corner when her mind registered what she had just seen. Barnaby! She spun around and ran back.

He sat on the railing, legs on the outside, with his arms spread wide.

Martha tackled him without hesitation, slung her arms around him, stepped against the railing and yanked Barnaby back with her full weight. He landed with his back on top of her. He struggled, he was strong, but she didn't let go. As she held him, held on to him, she realized that hot tears were streaming down her cheeks.

"Let go!" Barnaby shouted.

"You can't!" Martha screamed into his back. "You – you can't!"

"Let go of me!" He shouted again and finally managed to yank himself free. He scrambled away from her. Martha saw the confusion in his face but she was beyond pretense, she was beyond everything.

"You have to live," she cried up at him. "Don't you understand? You have to live!"

Wheezing, Bharad found them.

"Is everything all right?"

"Nothing is all right," Martha exclaimed. "Your friend tried to kill himself again."

"You did?" Bharad said. He stared at Barnaby, clearly upset and disappointed. Barnaby rose, dusted off his pants and tried to find the words.

"You have to let me go," he finally said.

Her eyes wide, Martha clapped her hands over her mouth as a wail tried to rise. She scrambled to her feet, eyes everywhere like an animal looking for a way out, then she ran off, her footsteps echoing for a while and finally disappearing.

# THERE IS NO DOCTOR ANYMORE

All for nothing, she thought. No progress, no hope, nothing. Everything that she had wished to be true, willed to be true, proved an illusion. Charles was right, Steward was right. Barnaby didn't want to fly, he wanted to die and the fact that she stopped him from doing so didn't really make her feel better, she realized. It could have been over. She could have followed him into the darkness of the sea. Moments of cold followed by peace.

She didn't respond to the tentative knock on the door. Not the first time, not the second time. She didn't want Bharad's help. She couldn't handle his warmth. Just when she thought he'd given up and gone away, the door opened.

Barnaby entered, looking uncomfortable. Something she hadn't seen from him before. He would be pensive, he would ignore and he would explode. A focus all his own as if the rest of the world didn't exist. Now he stood there, clearly ill at ease.

"Bharad said I should talk to you," he said at last.

Martha just looked at him, said nothing. The man who wanted to fly. The man who wanted to die. She wished she could say she didn't care anymore. He finally placed the one chair in the room as far from her as possible and sat.

"He told me about your son."

She rose abruptly from the bunk, facing away from him, looking out of the porthole. The sea was calm. She wasn't. She hadn't talked about it for a long time, had tried to bury it. But she knew she had to tell him, had to. She swallowed hard and began.       She told Barnaby about the day. That day. A completely ordinary day for the members of the Lewis family. She told him about her husband, their love for each other and for their only child Thomas. She told him about her son, his life, his friends, his hobbies. The perfectly regular happy world of Martha Lewis that had been.

"I followed Tommy that day. I don't know why, a sense, I don't know. I found him on the roof, near the edge. He wasn't crying. He was just - so sad ... I tried to talk to him. You know what he told me?"

Barnaby shook his head.

"Tommy said, 'I'm sorry, Mom. I'm not ready for all this ... life.' All this life. Then he jumped."

She turned to look at Barnaby. He was just sitting there in silence. Concentrated.

"There were no drugs, no alcohol, no bullying. No

indication, nothing. He was a happy child with a good life. A good life."

Her eyes stung, there were no more tears. She watched Barnaby rise and inch his way to the door. She suddenly lunged forward with big steps, reached him, grabbed his arm before he could make his escape. She stared at him.

"You have to live," she said, her pleading voice startling him.

He seemed lost for a moment, unsure of what he was supposed to do. He awkwardly pulled away from her grip and left the room.

~

Standing alone, hidden among the containers, Barnaby looked up at the sky. Seagulls caught his attention and his eyes followed them whenever they came into view.

"You have a responsibility now."

Barnaby turned to see Bharad standing there.

"No. I don't."

"You are a good person, Barnaby."

"I didn't ask for this."

"Life," Bharad said with a shrug and walked off.

That day something changed and it was Bharad who saw it most clearly. He saw two people, more courageous than he had ever seen them before. And it made him smile. That evening those two people sat next to him in the canteen. They ate in silence until all crew members had left. Finally, Barnaby looked up from his plate.

"I am sorry about your son."

Martha nodded.

"… You jumped from buildings nine times," she said. "Why didn't you die?"

"I don't know, Dr. Lewis."

"Please," she smirked, "Just Martha. There is no doctor anymore."

"… Martha." Barnaby said slowly, as if trying unknown food.

The following day Martha and Bharad went for a stroll on deck. She tried her best not to worry about Barnaby's whereabouts and she noticed that it was becoming easier. He wouldn't kill himself. Not now. Not after she had opened up. Not now that she was no longer his doctor but nothing more than a fellow traveler.

"We are making good time," Bharad said. "We should arrive in Mumbai tomorrow."

"Good. That's good. Do you know where Barnaby is?"

"Yes," he simply said and pointed up.

Martha looked up and saw Barnaby, standing high up on the roof of the captain's bridge. He stood, arms spread wide, motionless, in the midst of the many antennas up there. Martha was about to break into a run but Bharad held her back.

"Oh my God, we have to -"

"It's all right."

"How can you say that!? What if he jumps?"

"He will not jump," Bharad said.

"How can you be so sure?"

"Barnaby will not jump ... because of you, Dr. Lewis."

## NOTES FROM HIS DIARY

Life, Bharad had said. As if that would explain everything, anything. And maybe he was right. I told him that she wasn't my responsibility. I refused and he just smiled. Life. Martha. Desperate Martha Lewis. I was not going to take her weight. She was not the dog and I was not the old man in the story. I wouldn't be responsible for her, I kept telling myself. We so easily lie to ourselves. Today I know better. Even then I knew better.

She told me about her son and I felt him falling and I saw her broken heart. Bharad had pushed me into that, well knowing that I wouldn't be able to ignore it, well knowing that it was exactly what I needed. He just may have been the wisest person I have ever known. Yes, I would have killed myself that day. Yes, Martha saved my life … and I am grateful. Death is no longer an answer.

They gave me my freedom. No more restraints, no more supervision, I was left to roam the ship and I explored and discovered the winds from bow to stern. And with every touch of the salty breeze I felt stronger. I grew stronger than the death of my family, stronger than my pain, stronger than the darkness. I resolved to rise from it, fly high until darkness would be nothing but a disappearing dot far below. I resolved to live, once and for all.

In the 16th century there lived a young nun named Teresa. She was named a saint in time, Saint Teresa of Avila, and she would be forgotten had she not been an avid writer. Recording her time, her thoughts, her experiences. She levitated on several occasions throughout her life and recorded those moments she called "the rapture". She found those moments difficult, unpleasant and often tried to hold on to things to stop herself from lifting off the ground. "When I tried to resist these raptures," Teresa wrote, "it seemed that I was being lifted by a force beneath my feet so powerful that I know nothing to which I can compare it, for it came with a much greater vehemence than any other spiritual experience and I felt as if I were being ground to powder."

Why would anyone want to resist? She had it. The power of her mind. She simply didn't understand that it was her unconscious doing, her own ability. There was no act of God, there was her mind and oh what a mind Teresa must have had! She wrote "I can testify that after a rapture my body often seemed as light as if all weight had left it. Sometimes it was so noticeable that I could hardly tell when my feet were touching the ground again."

In those final days on the ship I felt that same lightness. As if I'd already flown. It made no sense to me. I had the weight of my memories, the faces of Vanessa and Aura, the horrors of a past that was, once more, perfectly clear. And there were Bharad and Martha. No, she was not my responsibility, regardless of how Bharad would look at me. Even now, she is not my responsibility. My life isn't hers. My goal isn't hers. But we walk the path together, for a while.

I felt light. Light. It is like the sweet scent of a rose. It is like the first glow of the morning sun. It is like looking into a pair of eyes and feeling your heart skip. It is every moment you've ever wanted to hold onto. I felt light. Whatever the reason, something was happening. Something that had to do with this journey. With Bharad. With Martha.

I would go with them. I would follow them on a journey that was theirs, not mine. Something was happening. And maybe we would even find that monk.


## IT'S GOOD TO HAVE FAMILY

The Pride of India was anchored at the edge of Mumbai's container harbor. Martha, Barnaby and Bharad had packed their few belongings and were ushered by a Turkish crew member to the far side of the ship, while custom officials boarded from the other.

Martha couldn't help it, she felt good. Despite the rushing and the dangers of being discovered, she felt better than she had in a very long time. She breathed in the scent of the orient, felt the heat of India on her skin. The Turk urged them on until they stood in front of Bharad's cousin Amit, looking sharp in a freshly starched uniform. A ladder led down to a small tugboat, waiting far below.

"I thank you, Cousin," Bharad said. "About the -"

"I do not want your money," the captain said. Bharad looked at him in surprise. "I may not be the worst of your cousins after all," Bharad's cousin added with a grin.

"You were listening." They embraced and broke off hurriedly when a crew member signaled a warning.

"Customs. Go now, quickly."

~

So this is India, Martha thought. The three of them stood on a sidewalk, traffic jam and market stands and people in every direction. It was chaotic, vibrant, colorful. Bharad told her that this place was called Crawford Market. She took a deep breath, smiled.

"It's beautiful."

"It's loud," Barnaby said.

Martha smirked and gave him a playful shove. Barnaby caught his balance and contorted his face into a return smile.

"He should have been here an hour ago but with this traffic ..." Bharad shrugged helplessly, Martha patted his shoulder.

"We're not in a hurry. How many cousins do you have, Bharad?"

"Twenty-one worldwide," he said. "Seven of them currently in Mumbai. Very useful! It's good to have family." The moment he said it, the moment he saw their faces, he regretted the words. "I am sorry."

"No, you're right," Martha said, smiling. "It is good to have family."

At that moment, a car's rhythmically honking horn caught their attention. A middle-aged man leaned from the driver's side window of a battered Jeep, waving wildly. Bharad's face split into a wide grin.

"Ajay! There he is. Come. Come!" he shouted at Martha and Barnaby and lunged into the traffic jam, weaving through cars, trucks and bikes. Martha saw him glow as he hugged Ajay with great affection. Bharad made the introductions and ushered them all into the relative safety of the car. Bharad joined his cousin in the front, Martha and Barnaby shared the back bench.

Martha saw the change in Bharad. From the moment

they had stepped onto Indian soil, he had smiled. A different smile. He had once told her that India didn't mean much to him … she could see just how wrong he had been. She watched him and Ajay, engrossed in a loud conversation in Hindi, full of laughter and exclamations. They inched through the traffic jam as horns honked, as mothers pulled their children, as vendors shouted and customers haggled. She saw spices on the tables, clothes and rugs and rows of cages, containing exotic birds of all sizes and colors. She noticed Barnaby glumly staring at the birds.

"How do you feel?" she asked. He didn't reply, didn't acknowledge her. "Barnaby. What are you thinking about?"

"St. Joseph's."

"That's behind you. Far behind."

"You used your credit card," Barnaby said.

"We needed more money," Martha explained. "It tells them that we came to Mumbai, nothing more. Believe me. They will never find us."

"I'm not going back there."

"You won't." She didn't know what else to say and was glad when Bharad turned his head, still glowing.

"It will be a bit bumpy, I'm afraid," he said and Ajay

laughed out loud.

"Don't worry," Ajay grinned, "After the first few hours you won't feel it anymore."

"How long will it take?" Martha asked.

"It is roughly two thousand kilometers to Kathmandu," Ajay said. "If all goes well you should get there in about thirty-five hours."

Ajay was right. As the Jeep bounced across a country road into the night, Martha didn't think about road conditions anymore. Behind them lay Mumbai and the last rays of the sunset. Ahead of them lay Kathmandu. She was too tired to think. Before she fell asleep, a final thought crossed her mind. It didn't register anymore, but it lingered.

What are you going to do when you get there, Martha?

## THE BIRD CALLS

They had stopped only when absolutely necessary and, just to be on the safe side, both Martha and Barnaby stayed out of sight whenever possible. They snuck into restrooms and they got to stretch their legs whenever

157

Ajay spotted an empty rest area.

It was more than a day later, night again and Barnaby was deep asleep, his face against the window. Martha looked out at endless stretches of darkness, occasional headlights, people, dogs, cows, carts. The dimly lit dashboard put a glow onto the faces of Ajay and Bharad. A tape played Hindu music and Ajay softly sang along. Bharad turned to face her.

"You should sleep, too," he said with a glance at Barnaby.

"I don't like my dreams," she replied.

"My wife died twenty-six years ago," Bharad softly said. "She is still in my dreams. She is always with me."

"... Does it ever get better?"

"She is my wife. He is your son. They are with us... and they smile." Bharad gave her a smile, looked at Ajay, listened to the music. "I love being home."

She closed her eyes and as she did, Bharad joined Ajay in song. A strange, haunting, melancholy song that transported her into sleep.

~

Martha woke when she felt the sun on her face. She

didn't open her eyes right away, realized that they were standing still. There were no voices, she was alone in the car. Martha squinted against the light and saw that they were parked at a rest stop in the middle of nowhere. Flatlands on one side of the road, jungle-like vegetation on the other.

Stepping out, she saw Ajay by a lone food stand. Bharad stood at a distance, facing the edge of the jungle. Barnaby stood by the car, watching Bharad. Martha joined him, stretching the stiffness from her limbs.

"Good morning," she said and Barnaby didn't reply, didn't even acknowledge her. Martha frowned. "Barnaby, are you all right?"

"He's just standing there," Barnaby said, always looking to Bharad.

"I don't see -"

"Listen," Barnaby interrupted.

Straining her ears, she picked up on a distant sound from within the lush vegetation beyond Bharad. At first she thought the deep guttural sounds were the calls of a monkey. It seemed as if all other sounds of the world had gone silent, there was only that recurring, eerie call. It was getting louder. It was coming closer. Closer to Bharad. Martha left Barnaby standing by the car, something was urging her forward.

Bharad's eyes were fixed on the forest and he hid the pain in his chest when he noticed Martha stepping next to him. The calls from within the trees didn't stop.

"What is it?" Martha asked quietly.

It was then that the big bird appeared. It was bigger even than a raven, all black except for wings that glimmered golden in the light and eyes that shone a piercing red. The bird called again, loud and deep, its head twitching in Bharad's direction with every sound.

"It is the Bharadwaj," Bharad said softly, "My namesake."

"It looks very special."

"They say," Bharad said, his eyes on the bird, "that the call of the Bharadwaj is an omen ... a bad omen."

Martha felt her throat closing up. Ridiculous. Omens. But she stood transfixed next to Bharad, both of them caught in the call of the bird.

"Shoo, shoo!" Ajay shouted.

Martha saw him hurrying over, carrying a tray filled with food and drink. He put the tray on the ground, reached for several rocks and threw them at the bird. The Bharadwaj angrily fluttered its golden wings before hopping off into the trees. They heard another call from within the jungle, then it was gone.

"Well, let us move on," Ajay laughed, overly cheerful. "We eat and drink in the car – Kathmandu is waiting!" He handed the tray to Martha and urged her on. When Martha looked back she saw him gently turning Bharad around, putting an arm around his shoulders and leading him back to the Jeep.

For a while Ajay tried to entertain, tried to banish the presence of the omen. Bharad assured him that everything was fine, but asked him to turn off the music so that he could rest a little.

He turned to Barnaby and Martha, looked at them with that singular smile of his, lightly nodded and went to sleep.

Moments later they heard him softly snore.

## NOTES FROM HIS DIARY

Bharad knew all the stories of India. He knew the gods and the tales. His wisdom allowed him to separate wealth from waste. And yet he chose to believe in the omen of that bird's call. It had rattled him, just as it had rattled Ajay. Why couldn't they believe in the opposite at least, why not believe that the bird signaled good fortune?

Is it a miracle when the blind begins to see and the lame begins to walk? Is it divine intervention when the incurable disease disappears into thin air? Why is it so much easier to believe in invisible gods, ghosts and magic? There are those who recognize that true power lies within the mind. They focus, truly focus … and suddenly things stop happening to them. They make things happen.

In our twenty-three years together, during all that time spent mostly inanimate, Bharad would share his stories. He would tell me stories I had researched many times before being committed, but he would also bring me new stories. He would glow when talking about the sages of India, ascetics, yogis who left the confines of small minds far below. There was one particular story that had been handed down from the Bharad's grandfather and he had passed it on to his children. They had shrugged it off – fairytales for simple people, they had said. In me, Bharad found a better listener.

Bharad's grandfather once invited a Tibetan lama into his home. The old man would tell the story over and over again and one final time on his death bed. He had heard about this lama and couldn't stop himself from asking –

would the guest show something of his powers? The lama smiled and asked for silence. Sitting in the lotus position, he took deep breaths until he inhaled one last time. Eyes focused on a place above him, he remained still as a statue for more than an hour. Not a single breath was taken, grandfather would assure young Bharad. Suddenly, the lama's body shivered and rose into the air. There he was, floating in the middle of the room, perfectly at ease. When the lama descended again, Bharad's grandfather profusely apologized. He had not intended to ask so much of the lama. The lama just smiled and said that it was nothing special, that most of his students were able to do what he had just done.

An Indian sage named Pantanjali described the path to levitation in the Yoga Sutras, an ancient text. But I have done the research, I have met the people and I know that human flight comes in many forms. Life-long study and meditation may be the path for some, their way is real – but it isn't the ultimate truth. The ultimate truth lies in simplicity. Life is simple. And equally simple it must be to unlock the mind. I don't want nirvana, I don't care about enlightenment. I just want to fly. I don't need one hundred and ninety-six sutras – all I need is a key to unlock that door.

Barnaby's face was turned away from her. Maybe he was sleeping, too.

"Barnaby?" she softly asked. He looked at her and waited. "What makes you so sure that flying is possible, Barnaby?"

He nodded as if he had waited for this question for a long time.

"It's not the hundreds of stories from every country, every age. It's not the research and the theories. It's a sense ... that has always been with me. Always."

"Mr. Merlin thought he once saw you levitate in the bird cage."

"I had dreamed of it," Barnaby said. "I had even told him about my dreams ... But it never happened."

There was no sadness in his voice, no regret and yet she could feel it, something. She took his hand and he allowed it. What are you doing, Martha? She had his hand in hers and it felt good. She didn't speak, just watched him as he searched for the right words.

"My entire life, I've felt so close to it. So close. So many times I've felt I was just a breath away from leaving the ground."

"Is life worth living, Barnaby?"

"... Yes."

Martha smiled. Barnaby didn't.

"We're one hour from Raxaul," Ajay announced loudly.

"Raxaul?" Martha asked.

"The border", he said with a bright smile. "The next leg of your adventure is about to begin." He shifted gears and the Jeep shot forward.

~

They arrived in a cloud of dust. It was late afternoon and the road to the border between India and Nepal was jammed with cars and buses, pick-ups and mule carts. Every mode of transportation packed with suitcases, cardboard boxes, crates and bundles.

Martha looked beyond the dust and the noise and spotted, up ahead, a white-washed customs building. Behind it the arch, flanked by two white towers. Get through there, Martha thought, and you're beyond anyone's reach. They won't find us. Ever. Martha frowned at her own thoughts.

Ajay drove the Jeep to the side of the road and

parked. He nudged the sleeping Bharad, nodded to Barnaby and Martha and got out. Ajay grabbed the duffel bags from the back and handed them to Barnaby and Martha before opening the door for Bharad.

"Cousin, I'm afraid this is where we must say good-bye."

Bharad didn't move.

"Bharad," Ajay said, grinning. He nudged his cousin, leaned in for a moment. He suddenly stepped back from the car. Far back.

"So how do we get across, Ajay?" When no response came, Martha turned and saw Ajay standing there as if he'd just seen a ghost. She saw him staring at Bharad and rushed forward. Bharad's skin was cool to the touch. Martha stayed near him, on her knees, for what seemed like a long time. The smile, that last smile she had seen, was still on his lips. When Martha stood, tears fell into the dust.

"He's dead," she said and looked to Barnaby. "I – I am so sorry."

Barnaby stared at her, blankly. He walked to the car, his steps big and fast. He knelt down next to Bharad, embraced him with all his might and didn't move anymore.

"What are we going to do?" Martha quietly asked Ajay.

He swallowed hard as he wiped tears from his eyes.

"My cousin told me that Barnaby was the most important person in his life." Ajay pointed in the direction of Nepal. "You must go on."

"But what about -"

"I will take Bharad back to his family in Mumbai. For the funeral," Ajay said.

"You can't drive all this way with a dead man."

"It will be my honor," Ajay simply said.

Martha was still lost in thought, wondering about how they could possibly continue without Bharad, when she saw Barnaby move. He took his knitted cap, gently placed it on Bharad's head and caressed his friend's cheek the way Bharad had always done with him. With a final glance Barnaby took his duffel bag and walked off, toward the border.

"Wait. Barnaby, wait," Ajay warned. He tried to take Barnaby's arm but Barnaby violently shook free and continued walking.

This was getting out of control fast and Martha felt utterly powerless. If the customs officers spot us, it's over, Martha thought. All over.

167

"Barnaby!" she called, trying to keep her voice down. Useless, he didn't listen. She turned to Ajay. "Help me, Ajay, please. If they stop us – what am I supposed to do!?"

"This is your journey," Ajay said, looking from Barnaby to Bharad. "If you make it across the border, take one of the buses. Five hours from now you will be in Kathmandu."

She felt like shaking Ajay, felt like screaming, but she knew he was right. It was her journey. He had to take care of family. Exasperated, she snatched up her duffel bag, hurriedly hugged Ajay and rushed off to catch-up with Barnaby.

Barnaby just kept marching, one step at a time, robot-like, toward the customs building. Martha caught up with him and forced herself to slow down. She tried to move Barnaby off course but he wouldn't give an inch.

"Barnaby," Martha whispered urgently. "I am as sorry as you are but if they catch us, all will have been in vain. Barnaby listen to me! Bharad wanted you to find that monk. He wanted you to fly. If we get caught now - !"

Nothing. It was as if he didn't hear. Barnaby just kept walking toward the customs officers up ahead. Martha watched them lazily inspect the passing carts and people.

There was no way Barnaby, tall and marching like a robot, wouldn't be noticed. Martha spotted one of the officers looking in their direction, frowning.

All of a sudden chaos erupted near them. Martha turned to see a cart full of caged chicken turning over and crashing to the ground. Amidst the people, shouting and laughing as chicken by the dozens fluttered in all directions, Martha saw Ajay running away. He gave her a final wave before vanishing in the crowd.

People will help, people will steal, people will gloat and many will simply stand and gawk.

As the many travelers chased every chicken that had tasted a moment of freedom, custom officers joined the hunt and Martha simply followed Barnaby, in a straight line, unhindered, across the border and into Nepal.

# CHAPTER THREE

# FINDING THE MONK

# NOTES FROM HIS DIARY

Bharad had told me many times about his weak heart, about his visits to the doctor, about the fear that he might not always be there to care for me. He's gone now – and he didn't die of a weak heart. Superstition killed him. A bird, an omen. Bharad let that happen. Why did he choose to die?

I cannot describe what happened that day. Bharad was dead. My friend, my best friend, my only friend – gone. I didn't hear Martha, I just walked and I barely noticed the people around me, the noise, the cars, the dust in the air. I just walked. I don't think I intended to walk across the border, I just needed to be in motion. And when I came to my senses we were in Nepal. I sat and waited and Martha took care of everything.

I should thank her. Maybe I'll learn to speak again, a real conversation – just two people in the comfort of each other's company. I could speak with Vanessa, about everything, and it was good. But that was then. The words won't come now and when they do they come out wrong. I really should thank Martha.

That last time Bharad looked back at me, at Martha, he knew that he would never see us again. He knew that he would close his eyes forever. Sometimes, right now, I wish that there were spirits, an afterlife. What if. I wish I could see my family again. I wish I could see Bharad again. He must have known that I loved him. He must have.

From then on it was just me and Martha. And we've been together ever since. Weeks now. Close. She is not my responsibility, Bharad. She's not. Two people, two journeys – parallel, not together.


## I BELIEVE IN YOU

When Martha returned, she saw Barnaby still stoically sitting on a bench next to Nepalese and Indians, holding on to his duffel bag, staring straight ahead. She glanced in every direction, at every face. Nobody seemed to care about these two white faces.

"I have tickets," she told Barnaby. "We leave in thirty minutes."

Barnaby gave the slightest of nods. The wrinkled old Nepalese man sitting next to Barnaby gave Martha a toothless smile. He roughly shoved the people to his right further across and encouraged Martha to squeeze in between himself and Barnaby. She nodded her thanks and sat.

"Well, we're in Nepal," she said.

Barnaby stayed still as a statue.

"I miss him, too," she added. "He left you something."

Barnaby slightly turned his head and focused on her. Martha unzipped her duffel bag, reached into it and pulled out the blue photo album Bharad had shown her. It seemed an eternity since that time at Bharad's home, when they had talked and read and mused in the cramped little guest room, exploring the world of Barnaby together. Martha handed the book to Barnaby. He just held it in his hands.

"It's mine," he said.

"Bharad kept all your things from the time before St. Joseph's. He wanted me to give it you." Martha watched Barnaby closely.

"Thank you," he finally muttered.

"… He wrote something."

Barnaby frowned at her as he opened the album. On the inside of the cover was Bharad's handwritten note.

*I believe in you.*

*Your friend, Bharad*

Barnaby's fingers traced the letters.

He took a deep breath and opened the album's first page. He gingerly went from page to page, pictures of clouds, his pictures. Abruptly, he shut it again. Martha saw him fighting emotion, containing it, willing it back, down, away.

"These pictures," Martha gently said, "you took them on special days?" He nodded, almost against his will. "Show me," she said.

Barnaby opened the album again. He looked at a dozen photographs and Martha saw that every shape of every cloud had a meaning for him. A smile spread across his face as he stopped at the photograph of a dark sky and brilliantly white cloud formations before it. The light before the storm.

"The day our daughter was born," Barnaby said.

~

Another night, another bumpy one. Martha dozed off occasionally. Whenever she woke, she saw variations of the same, a narrow road snaking higher and higher, past rocks and huts and temples. There were occasional dots of light in the night, on hills as black as the sky. She didn't see a single star. Everyone in the bus was asleep – everyone except for Barnaby. When she woke another time, Martha realized her head was nudged into his shoulder. He didn't seem to mind and Martha went back to sleep.

It was light outside when Martha opened her eyes again. Confused, she looked around – she was alone in the bus. Passengers stood on the road up ahead. She rubbed her face and exited the bus. The road was blocked, caused by the crash of two buses. One of them lay there on its side, like the carcass of a large animal.

Martha saw Barnaby standing apart from the others. As she walked to him, the passengers combined their strengths, leaned against the bus and heaved and yelled until the bus stood upright again. They laughed and applauded and one of them, clearly the driver, went from person to person, expressing his gratitude with a long series of bows.

"Why didn't you wake me?" Martha asked.

"We're almost there," Barnaby replied, pointing down. Far below, nestled into a valley surrounded by mountains, lay a vast city.

"Kathmandu," Martha said, her voice hushed as if they'd just discovered Shangri-La.

"He's down there somewhere," Barnaby said.

"Barnaby," Martha cautioned, "A city that size – don't expect too much. It may take a long time to find this monk."

"I will find him," he said with conviction.

Martha smiled and put his hand in his. They stood there, next to each other, and Martha realized once again that she hadn't thought it through to the end. So far, everything had worked. Barnaby was alive and awake. The journey, the quest, giving him a purpose. But she had never expected to find that monk. She was pretty sure he didn't even exist. And if he did exist he was bound to be a real person with as much of an ability to fly as she had. Life is good, Barnaby had agreed. He saw that now. Life was worth living ... and Martha fervently hoped that, over time, Barnaby would realize that finding that monk wouldn't matter anymore. He will let it go. He will move on, Martha thought, feeling the warmth of his hand in hers. But when Barnaby spoke again, Martha struggled to keep her smile in place.

"I will find him," he said again. "And when I do, I will fly."

## KATHMANDU DREAMING

It was a moment she would never forget. Not because of something that happened but simply for the fact that they were there. Barnaby and Martha, duffel bags in hand, stood side by side in front of the imposing white dome of the Boudhanath Temple. It had started with a crazy idea. Implausible, impossible. Had she ever really believed that they would make it all the way to Kathmandu? Well, they had … and she sent silent thanks to Bharad.

Bharad. As much as his death had been a shock, she had the oddest sensation that he was with them, still. She couldn't see him, not like she had seen her dead son for months after his death, but she felt him. He was there and he gave her strength. He would know what to do now … Martha didn't.

The streets around the temple were busy on this clear day, the countless prayer flags shivered in the wind, vendors called for tourist groups to visit their stands, monks passed by like ghosts. Martha noticed that Barnaby's search had already begun. His eyes everywhere, he spotted an elderly monk and walked off. Martha sighed and followed Barnaby. The real quest was only just beginning.

The following weeks were both intense and light, frustrating and uplifting. There was something about the people of Kathmandu, about the streets, the air, the language, everything around them, that made her feel welcome here. Martha mapped the city with Barnaby, planned searches, recorded conversations and statements. She went with him most often but found herself trusting him more and more. Sometimes they just sat at a corner, watching people passing by for hours. Often Barnaby would jump to his feet, try to get information from someone, trying to offer them money. He was surprisingly fast in picking up bits and pieces of the local language, Nepali.

They had rented an apartment near Boudhanath Temple and one day, as Martha pulled up the blinds, she found that the apartment had become their home. The blue photo album had a special place on a dresser. The already furnished apartment had a far more lived-in look now. Local paintings on the walls next to a large map of

Nepal with lots of pins and notes detailing the status of the search for the mysterious monk. There were new curtains, bright rugs, fresh flowers and a kitchen that both felt and was rich with spices.

She wouldn't have admitted it to anyone but she couldn't lie to herself, not anymore. She liked this place, she liked her life ... and she liked Barnaby Smith.

She marveled at his relentless intensity. She loved watching him when his eyes followed the birds. She found herself laughing and joking with him during their dinners as they planned their next searches. The children in their neighborhood got to know him. They had observed him talking to monks, or trying to, flapping his arms as if they were wings and soon they called him 'crazy bird'. And when he was out, in the dark, in the rain, searching, always searching, she found herself missing him.

Heavy rain battered against the windows as Barnaby came in, soaked to the bone. Martha, preparing dinner in the kitchen, peeked around the corner.

"Dinner's almost ready."

"I'm going to Kapan," Barnaby said, walking to the map. Martha walked in, removed his drenched coat and cap.

"What's in Kapan?"

"A temple. He's been seen there." Martha smiled and hung up the coat, trying her best to appear casual. It was probably nothing. None of the leads had brought them any closer to finding anything, or anyone, unusual.

"Kapan. Good. Now let's eat." He sat down, still deep in thought, still looking at the map. Martha put down two steaming plates and joined him. She poured wine, tasted it, handed him a glass and raised hers. "To Kathmandu."

Barnaby drank, ate, eyes still on the map.

"Beyond Kapan is Helambu, Martha. Maybe that's where -"

"Yes, Barnaby," she said with a light smile. "Maybe. It's one of the many possible places. We've only been here seven weeks, Barnaby. It'll take time."

He still stared at the map, the many dots, the endless unexplored possibilities. He was clearly frustrated and Martha patted his hand.

~

After dinner Barnaby did what he always did in the evenings. He wrote. Upon noticing his first frustrations,

Martha had bought a small diary for Barnaby. She had handed him the leather-bound book after their second week in Kathmandu and told him to write – anything he wanted. He had smiled when he saw the book – it had the shape of a bird in flight imprinted on the cover.

Ever since he would sit there, every night. He would sit and stare at the wall, he would write slowly, he would look at Martha and look away again. Sometimes he would add a page, a sentence, a single word – and sometimes he would just sit there, with the diary, seemingly lost in thought. As much as she longed to know what he was writing about, she never went close to the diary. That was his world, his thoughts.

She saw that the writing was doing him good. It always seemed to calm him down after spending his days searching in vain. As Martha put the dinner plates away, she glanced at Barnaby and smiled.

## NOTES FROM HIS DIARY

The morning I first saw the city, looking down at it, I felt something that I can't explain. It was as if I were coming home. As if Kathmandu was exactly where I needed to be. That morning, when Martha held my hand, I realized that I really did have to find that monk. All of this has been born of a desperate woman's crazy idea.

Martha has brought me to this place for her own reasons and I know this is where I need to be. I choose to believe in this monk. I choose to find him. I choose to make it happen. I can feel her looking at me. She is ... doing well. Happy, perhaps. She is with me, she helps me, she found the apartment and does everything she can to make this a home. She plays family – for my sake, for her sake. She is a very smart woman. She knows that this strange dream of hers can't last. I am not her salvation. I am Barnaby Smith, the man who will fly.

Seven weeks. Only seven weeks, Martha says. In these seven weeks we have watched and waited. We focused on major temples first, on Boudhanath, Taleju, Ashok Binayak, Shiva, Maju, Narayan, Shiva-Parvati, Bhagwati, Saraswati, Krishna, Kal Bhairab, Indrapur, Vishnu and Mahendreswar. We circled the temples, asked around and followed monks. I began to understand the people, the language, the faces. They know something but nothing is spoken. I keep asking and keep watching their eyes and little by little I make connections. A frown here, a twitch there, they won't say but they know something. This monk is more than a myth. He does exist.

Martha doesn't believe in any of this but she humors me. She waits for me to give up, for my quest to end, for the moment when I see life as she does. Sometimes I have to walk away and swallow my anger. She is content, here, with me. How could she be – how can she want this to be real? I wish I could talk to her but I wouldn't know what to say any more than I know what to write. I will not lose my patience.

I have widened the circles across Kathmandu and the villages beyond and I see a pattern now. The faces, the frowns, the eyes, spoken and unspoken denials. Nobody has ever heard of such a monk. A flying monk. They smile politely, they call it a nice story, a myth, no more than that. But I see beyond their lies. I see the fear in their eyes. The monk is real. No, I will not lose my patience. I will not give up.

I will find the monk. He is real. Real.

# AND THEN HE WAS GONE

Another day, another search. Martha knew it couldn't last. Knew it wasn't right. She had built herself an illusion, rich and warm with every facet feeling right.

And yet she knew she couldn't allow this to continue forever. At some point she would have to tell him, straight out, that she had just been playing along. A constant lie to keep the illusion of their life in Kathmandu alive.

Martha exchanged a few words in Nepali with an old woman selling fruit. They smiled at each other and the woman also nodded politely at Barnaby who stood right behind Martha, carrying shopping bags.

He was losing hope and Martha knew it.

She would be there, by his side. She had brought him this far, she would get him through this, too.

It happened without warning. Barnaby dropped the bags and ran.

"Barnaby? Barnaby!"

Not wasting a moment to explain, she left everything she had with the old woman and chased after Barnaby. There he was, in the crowd, not far ahead but too far to shout. All she could do was try to catch up.

There he was, far ahead, around a corner, pushing and shoving, there, gone again. For a glimpse, she thought she saw past Barnaby, saw the orange robe of a monk disappearing around the corner.

Barnaby rushed after it.

Moments later Martha ran around the corner and froze.

A dead end.

A dead end exactly like the one she had described when telling the story on the ship. Barnaby just stood there, out of breath, wide-eyed, shocked.

"Barnaby, what is it?" Martha said, approaching him slowly, speaking soothingly, hands raised, calming.

"The monk. He was here."

"There's nobody," Martha said, rattled.

"Exactly!"

"Sometimes … sometimes we see what we want to see."

"He was here," Barnaby replied angrily.

"I believe you."

"No, you don't," Barnaby hissed at her, furious. "You're just happy if I run around in circles for the rest of my life. This is not living - not for me!"

"Barnaby, I -"

187

"You are not my doctor. And I am not your son," Barnaby said and walked away.

Martha remained behind, the walls of the dead end closing in on her, spinning around her.

There goes the illusion, Martha.

Watch it all disappear.

Gone.


## THE TREK TO HELAMBU

Barnaby sat on the steps of Boudhanath Temple beneath one of the white elephant statues. It was late night and the prayer flags up above rattled in the wind as if whispering secrets. He was alone, knees pulled up, staring at the ground.

When he saw sandals in front of him, and the hem of an orange robe, Barnaby looked up. There stood a teenage boy, fifteen perhaps, evenly looking at Barnaby.

"You come here much. You like Boudhanath Temple."

Barnaby said nothing.

"You are lost," the boy continued and it was no question.

"I want to be alone," Barnaby mumbled.

"I understand," the boy said and sat down next to Barnaby.

Annoyed, Barnaby glanced at him but the boy didn't seem to notice. He just sat there, knees pulled up like Barnaby, looking straight ahead. And so they sat there in silence, together.

~

Martha didn't look up when Barnaby walked in the next morning. It was the first light of day and Martha, dressed in hiking gear, finished stuffing her backpack.

"Where are you going?" he asked.

"Helambu," she said.

"... Why?" he asked.

She stopped packing, took a deep breath. Barnaby looked worn, tired, worried. Right at that moment Martha didn't care. She had been up all night, too. She had wrestled with her own demons, punched them into the recesses of her mind and had decided to fight. She was going to fight for Barnaby, with Barnaby, whatever the cost.

"I am not your doctor and you're not my son," she said calmly.

He tried to speak but she raised her hand.

"If that monk really does exist," Martha said, "I will help you find him."

Barnaby looked at her, frowning.

"If we find him, I will jump."

"We'll see," she said with a shrug and continued packing.

"I will jump," he said forcefully.

"We don't have all day," she replied.

As she tied her hiking boots, she saw him going for his gear. He kept giving her sideways glances. He was no doubt wondering about her ... and so was she, wondering what she was bargaining for. But despite the uncertainty of what the coming days would bring, Martha felt stronger, better.

She was done lying.


## NOTES FROM HIS DIARY

There was a boy, a boy monk. He sat with me at the temple, through the night, that last night in Kathmandu. I didn't ask for company and yet he gave it. We didn't speak for most of the time, we didn't need to. He seemed to know me and I'm sure that was just my imagination. He was simply … there.

Children. Young minds. If we could harness their powers, if we could retain that abundance of power as we become adults. Most children lose it all the moment they are bombarded by the reason of small minds. They're told to stop acting childish. They're told to sit straight, to fit in and to be quiet. They're told that they're an embarrassment, that they need to adjust and play along. Why can't you be like everyone else, they're told.

There's a body of research focused on the minds of young children. And there is an abundance of stories of children in flight. Before they're told what's possible and what's not, they float up and down stairs, they levitate across ponds, they fly around buildings. And no one believes them. They were just dreaming, day-dreaming with that over-active imagination of theirs. That silly child. Stop dreaming. Grow up. So much potential going to waste because of small minds.

The young monk was with me until morning broke and I felt that I had to go see Martha. To do what, I didn't know. I wouldn't apologize, I couldn't. I had spoken the truth. I just felt that she shouldn't be alone. As it turned out, I was wrong about her. Maybe desperation will do that for you. It can kill you, it can lock you in a prison of tears – or it can make you stronger. When I returned to the apartment that morning, Martha was different. She was daring me, daring herself. She dares to come with me into the mountains - it must be like bringing her own son up to that roof.

I find myself caring about Martha. It's not as it was with Vanessa but something's there and I don't want it. I will not be weighed down.

## TWO WHITE COFFINS

Two white coffins, one of them child-sized, in the middle of Brooklyn's Green-Wood Cemetery. The funeral of Vanessa and Aura Smith didn't attract a large gathering. Just a few people stood by as a priest spoke. Barnaby didn't hear the words, didn't pay attention to the faces of the people around him.

His wife was dead. His daughter was dead. Storks. Tractor. Death. But not Barnaby. Barnaby Smith was alive. Why don't you die? He had his face raised, his eyes up in the tree, up in the clouds, up there with the passing birds.

Barnaby realized that he was crying, that Mr. Merlin hugged him fiercely, that Vanessa's parents uttered gruff condolences. He turned away from everyone and walked away, alone, alone again. The tears kept flowing but he didn't feel them. He felt something else.

Looking up again, at the clouds, at a flock of pigeons.

Something felt … good. As he kept walking, he looked down at his shoes.

They seemed to barely touch the grass.

~

"What are you telling me?" Martha asked, looking back at Barnaby. They were hiking up a dusty track, through a lush deep green countryside.

"I'm telling you how I felt."

"Light?" she asked with another glance back. He nodded.

"Light."

Martha let it go. The burden of responsibilities, the weight of compromise, life. She was done analyzing. She just kept walking and he just kept following and they didn't speak another word. When they reached a fork in the dirt track, Martha stopped. It was late afternoon and they'd have to find a place to stay for the night before long. There were a few huts up on a hill with the white mountains looming in the distance.

Martha drank from her water bottle, passed it on to Barnaby. She felt the sweat dripping down her back and cooling fast as she unhooked the backpack and reached for the map. We could be anywhere, she thought, looking at the map.

"You are on right path," a voice said and Martha was startled to see a young monk standing in front of her. He was dressed in a traditional orange robe and carried nothing but a small shoulder bag.

"Oh, hello," Martha said. "You speak English, wonderful. Maybe you can help? We are looking for -"

"Flying monk," the boy said. He winked and smiled at Barnaby.

"How do you -?" Martha began - and stopped when she saw the look on Barnaby's face. "You two know each other?"

"We have met," Barnaby replied.

"I am Ram," the young monk said with a bow, took the left fork of the track and swiftly marched uphill.

"You know where we can find the flying monk?" Barnaby called after him.

"Yes. Come!"

Barnaby and Martha shot each other a glance, quickly shouldered their backpacks and hurried after the boy.

## BEWARE OF THE WIND

The stars, so many of them. Martha had never seen such a brilliance of sky.

They had walked on for a long time, into the night, and now they were huddled around a small fire, sheltered from the wind by giant boulders.

She had wandered into the darkness, away from the fire, to take in the stars. But the cold soon pulled her back to the fire where Barnaby and Ram sat, close to each other, in silence.

"You're not cold?" Martha asked as she joined them again.

"I think warm, I am warm," Ram said with a smile.

"Tell me about the monk," Barnaby said.

"His name is Akash," Ram began. Even the name seemed to frighten the young monk. "It means sky," he added.

Barnaby watched the boy's face.

"Do you know him? Personally?"

"No," Ram said, "only hear. He is dangerous man."

"If he's so dangerous," Martha asked, "Why are you taking us to him?"

Ram looked at her and pointed at Barnaby.

"It is his wish," Ram said and continued, "Do you know Yeti?"

"Yes, of course," Martha replied.

"Yeti not real. Akash real."

As if on cue a violent gust of wind rushed through the cracks between the boulders, rattled the flames and was gone again. Ram looked around, waited for the flames to settle before continuing quietly.

"Akash does not like people. You stay by fire. Not walk away."

With this the boy curled up and closed his eyes.

Martha looked at Barnaby, his face glowing with the light of the flames. He wanted to believe, she knew that.

But did he?

Did he believe these stories by a boy who just happened to appear, who volunteered to be their guide, who ever so conveniently claimed to know that elusive monk?

"I don't trust him," Martha whispered.

"He is a monk," was all that Barnaby said as if that

clarified everything. She shook her head, crawled into her sleeping bag and watched Barnaby.

He remained seated.

He looked content.

"Good night, Barnaby."

"Good night, Martha."

~

When Martha opened her eyes again, the fire was still strong and, beyond the flames, Ram smiled at her. She shook Barnaby awake and was surprised to find that Ram had even made them some type of bread paddy, fresh off a hot stone he'd used as a makeshift frying pan. The boy didn't seem in a hurry to get going, it was Barnaby who rushed them forward, convinced he'd soon meet his destiny.

Once again Ram led the way, and Barnaby and Martha often struggled to keep up. Sometimes the boy would disappear and they'd eventually see him, high up, sitting on a rock, meditating. Like now. There he was, sitting on a rock, waiting for them. I need a rest, a bed, Martha thought miserably.

"We arrive Helambu today. Evening," Ram

announced.

"And Akash?" Barnaby asked.

"Two more days."

"How did you find us, Ram?" Martha probed.

"It is my path," he shrugged.

High up in the clouds they heard a noise. Too small for airplanes, too big for birds. Three colorful tiny planes hummed across the sky.

"Ultra-lights," Barnaby muttered.

"Not real flying," Ram said.

"No," Barnaby agreed, "Not real flying."

Martha looked from Barnaby to the boy. Both of them with their thoughts way up there. One a man who had always wanted to fly like a bird, a man who, despite the countless scars and broken bones, still believed. The other a boy who claimed to know a mystical monk with the sky as his name and the wind as his voice. Flying is impossible, she felt herself thinking for the millionth time. Flying is impossible. So why did she still feel compelled to ask?

"Ram. Do you really think Akash can fly?"

"Bird flies," Ram said.

"Birds have wings."

"Wind flies," he replied, turned and marched on.

There they go, Martha thought. Barnaby already on Ram's heels again. Martha stood there, looking up the hiking trek, beyond Barnaby, beyond Ram, to the white mountains beyond. She sighed and knew she wouldn't give up, wouldn't ever stop.

Over the course of the next twenty-four hours she shivered and laughed, struggled and gaped and realized she wouldn't want to be anywhere else but right here in the company of her two most unlikely companions.

Ram showed them springs and introduced them to villagers. He taught them to fly kites with the children of the village. They were given food, smiles and pats on their shoulders and when Martha looked back she saw them talking to each other, shaking their heads. Long after the village had disappeared far below them, the climbing continued. The wind rose and the weather worsened. Martha struggled with every step, Barnaby grit his teeth and finally, finally Ram pointed to a small hut nestled into the rocks.

They reached the barren structure just before the storm broke. Howling winds tore at the walls but they were solid enough to allow for a small fire to rise and light up the room. Exhausted, both Barnaby and Martha were soon in their sleeping bags – but sleep wouldn't come. Ram sat by the glow of the fire, meditating.

"Bad weather," Martha softly said.

Ram opened his eyes.

"Akash. He know we are here."

"All these stories about him ..." Barnaby said, "Ram ... are they real?"

The wind rattled the roof and Ram closed his eyes again.

"Wind is voice of Akash. Not listen. Not go outside. Sleep."

Martha looked at Barnaby and tried a smile she didn't feel.

The wind howled, tearing through the cracks in the walls, biting, trying to hurt. It had something powerfully hypnotizing. The voice of Akash, like a demon's hungry scream ... Martha tried to shake the idea but the feeling remained. Coming here, into the middle of nowhere, had never felt more wrong than it did right at that moment.

# NOTES FROM HIS DIARY

I may not continue this journal. My hands are freezing, the pen barely works. I write in the glow of the fire. Martha is asleep, her face alive in the shadows of flickering flames. I find myself smiling.

The boy lies by the rattling door. He might be sleeping, too, but I don't think so. He is guarding us. From whatever is out there, the wind, Akash. Ram, our protector from the danger we have come here to find. It doesn't make sense, he doesn't make sense. And yet here we are, in his company.

This monk … Akash. What if we find him? What if we actually find him? I've come too far to stop. I could step outside now, push the boy aside and walk to the edge of the cliff. I could jump right now. Maybe this is the time. But I look at Martha and I hesitate. I remember my wife and my child and I hesitate. I wish my thoughts were like a page in this book. Something I could just tear out and burn. But the opposite is happening, these thoughts, these images, they're getting stronger. They fill me up and pull me down, chain me to the ground. I need to meditate, somehow, prepare for this monk.

I'm questioning everything and it's her fault and it's

my fault. I should have known better. She shouldn't be here. This is my journey, my quest. Martha, desperate Martha. She's stronger with every step we take … and with every step I become more uncertain. Uncertainty will kill me. The boy lies in the shadow by the door, he doesn't stir. Maybe he really is asleep. That wonderful calm. That is what I need. That calm.

Martha sleeps and a memory crawls through her. A shiver, a frown, then she lies still again. What is she dreaming about? What are you dreaming about, Martha? She smiles now … and I smile.

Ram is guiding us … but I am lost.


## THE EDGE OF THE CLIFF

Bharad's smiling face.

He sat on a rock, next to a black bird with golden wings and red eyes. She was terrified. Someone was pushing her, forward, toward the abyss before her. Martha shot a glance over her shoulder and recognized Barnaby.

He was pushing her and he was smiling like Bharad. She tried to get away but he grabbed her, pushed her

202

again. One step from the edge, one more push. Martha woke with the dream still lingering, her mouth dry from a silent scream.

She sat straight up, eyes wide open.

There was no wind.

Daylight streamed in narrow slivers through the cracks of roof and walls. No Barnaby. No Ram.

For an instant, she felt a stab of pain in her chest. They've left me. They've abandoned me because they know I'm a fake. Why don't you believe, Martha? What if, Martha, what if? Suddenly she rushed to her feet and ran from the hut into the blinding sun.

"Barnaby!" she shouted into the white.

No reply but her own voice, echoing from far away. She rubbed her eyes, shielded them and early morning came into focus. Looming mountains, some still dark in the shadows. Clouds covering many of the peaks. Barnaby standing by the edge of a cliff ...

"Barnaby!" she shouted again and ran.

He turned, saw her hurtling toward him, his face didn't change.

It was calm, too calm. She stopped a few feet away from him.

"Please come away from the edge."

He didn't move. She stepped closer.

"He's gone," Barnaby said.

"What are – Ram? Ram is gone?" Barnaby nodded. "He left us here in the middle of nowhere? How are we supposed to –"

Fear ripped the words from her throat when Barnaby suddenly pulled her to the very edge of the cliff. He simply pointed down.

Far below, impossible to reach, Martha discovered the tiny figure of Ram, crushed between rocks. She felt the wind increase, rushing in her ears, into her mind, into her stomach. She heard the fall, the sounds of her son dying. Martha rocked back and forth, almost fell and Barnaby grabbed her hard. He pulled her back and sat her down on a rock, at a safe distance from the cliff.

"Oh God, no … I …" Martha screamed in agony but nothing escaped.

She ran over the edge but stayed in place.

A voice in the back of Martha's head calmly said 'You should be used to this by now. Another day, another death. Get over it, Martha.'

"I woke up," Barnaby said, standing before her, looking uncomfortable. "Ram wasn't there. I went looking for him."

"... How could that have happened?"

"He told us not to go out at night. Maybe he did."

"That's crazy," Martha said as she tried to control her breathing. "... This Akash is no evil spirit. He's not the wind, he's just a monk - those are just stories, Barnaby."

"Like flying?" Barnaby asked.

Martha buried her head in her hands again.


# PENNE ALL'ARRABIATA

They packed in silence, rolled up their sleeping bags, forced themselves to eat and drink. It had taken time. They had moved like sleepwalkers. It was two hours after the discovery of Ram. They were ready.

"I'm pretty sure we can find our way back to Helambu," Martha said when Barnaby kept staring at the map in his hands. A few places were marked there, the road from Kathmandu through Kapan and Helambu – and a final circle with the name 'Latang'. Barnaby tucked the map away, shouldered his pack and walked – up the steep path.

"Barnaby," Martha shouted at his back, exasperated. "We don't know the way. There's no one out there. We either starve or freeze to death."

Barnaby stopped and looked back at her.

"You're right. You should go back."

Martha stared at him in disbelief.

"You'd like that, wouldn't you? All on your own. Free ... light." She shouldered her pack, her face hard, and marched past him. "I'm not going to make it that easy for you." When she looked back, he still stood there, frowning. "What are you waiting for?"

He lightly shook his head and followed.

That night Martha secretly cursed her decision to continue ... until she didn't. They were nestled into a narrow cave beneath a looming rock, both in their sleeping bags. Martha was weak, dead tired and staring at nothing.

"I bet Steward is still looking for us," she said. "Maybe one day he'll find our bones ... right here."

"... I did say I would kill you," Barnaby said.

"Yes, I remember," Martha replied. "Why did you say it?"

"I wanted you to scare you. I wanted you to leave me alone."

"... I guess you didn't scare me enough," Martha said.

They sat in silence against the back of the cave, a space between them. Barnaby moved in his sleeping bag and closed the gap. It was surely imaginary but Martha felt the warmth. She smiled.

~

Certain death. Those two words were swirling through her frozen mind like the occasional snowflakes that flickered past her line of sight.

Martha and Barnaby had marched on and were more lost than ever before. She knew it and he ignored it as the wind kept tearing at them. Martha sneered at it.

That all you got, Akash? She didn't care anymore. If Barnaby continued, she would follow. That's all there was, his backpack, his shoes, step after step.

Just stay with him.

Step.

Just keep climbing.

Step.

We're both crazy, she thought. All of this ... insane. She saw Bharad walking next to Barnaby. You're hallucinating, Martha. When she stumbled she cracked her knee. Pain shot through her and snapped her back into harsh reality. Barnaby stepped back and helped her to her feet.

They were bundled to their noses but she could see a smile in his eyes. She smiled back. Yes. We're both crazy. He put his arm around her and walked her straight up to a bolder the size of a house.

The bolder shielded them from the wind. She took the map from Barnaby, unfolded it and had it torn from her hands instantly. A gust of wind blew it away and she just shook her head. No point in chasing it. She sat down and pulled the shawl from her face.

Finished. This is the end.

"For all we know we could be in Tibet by now," she said, a strange sense of giddiness rising up in her. Barnaby didn't seem to hear. He looked up at the peaks, watched the birds flying in wild circles and daring dives. "I'd really like a steaming hot plate of penne all'arrabbiata right about now. With a bottle of Brunello di Montalcino. That would really make my day. Barnaby, what would you …"

She realized only then that he had walked away to the side of the bolder. He stood there, transfixed, and slowly turned to her.

"Martha. Look."

She struggled to her feet, leaned on him before

looking up. They saw a little monastery, high up, clawed into the middle of a sheer cliff. A narrow path was visible and Martha didn't have to look at Barnaby to know that his eyes were glowing.

## THE JOURNEY'S END

It was as if the wind was trying to hold them off, keep them away, tear them off the path and sweep them down into the rocks below – but despite their exhaustion, they reached the small plateau that offered just enough ground for two small brick buildings and a miniscule yard leading up to them. The tiny monastery, more like a hermitage, in fact, seemed to greet them with the many fluttering prayer flags.

When Barnaby and Martha reached the plateau the howling wind gave way to a pleasant breeze. It just feels this way, Martha thought, there's nothing supernatural here. This spot was simply chosen because it is sheltered from the currents, a quiet haven. Looking up gave her vertigo, looking down did the same. On her left a vertical cliff rose into the clouds. On her right the equally sheer cliff rushed down into nothing. They both stood, staring at the closed door of the monastery.

"End of the quest," Barnaby said.

"Maybe there's no one up here," Martha said, hoping against hope.

When the door opened, they both gaped in surprise. It was Ram standing there. He hurriedly closed the door and rushed to join them.

"Ram!" Martha shouted.

He gave her a quick smile that instantly disappeared again.

"Please you must go," he said.

"We thought you were dead," Martha said. "We —"

"A trick," Barnaby said and Ram nodded.

"It is my duty."

"Stories and tricks to keep people away from here," Barnaby said.

"I told you. Master Akash does not like people. Please, go."

"Barnaby …" Martha gently reached for his arm but he pulled away from her, his focus fully on the monastery.

"Can he really fly? Tell me."

"It does not matter," Ram replied. "If you stay, you will die."

"We should go, Barnaby. Please," Martha urged and Ram agreed.

"Yes, please go."

Barnaby looked from Ram to Martha. He hesitated. Martha saw her chance to reach him before it was too late.

"Barnaby. I, I wanted you to find your life – not end it." She could see him wavering and finally she said what she had long known to be the truth.

"You are all I have," she added.

Before she had a chance to go on, a gust of wind tore past them, through them, and slammed open the monastery door.

There he stood – Akash.

The monk evenly looked at them. Then he pointed at Barnaby and motioned for him to come in. Barnaby looked to Martha, to Ram, their eyes telling him to walk away. Barnaby wiped a tear from Martha's cheek. His mind made up, he stepped forward and walked past the monk into the monastery.

Akash looked at Martha, lightly bowed and closed the door.

Martha just stood and stared. They were here. They had found the monk. This monk actually existed and

Martha remembered what Barnaby had said. "I will find him. And when I do, I will fly."

Martha barely noticed that Ram pulled her to the side and sat with her against the side of the mountain. Martha's eyes remained on the monastery.

"People come here before," Ram said, "They want to fly."

"What happened to those people?" Martha asked and knew she wouldn't like the answer when Ram pointed over the edge of the cliff.

"They are down there."

Martha shook her head in anger, rose abruptly.

"We have to do something."

"I cannot," Ram said weakly.

"You led us here!"

"You came here," the young monk replied.

~

The monk sat on the ground in a lotus position, his eyes closed. Barnaby sat opposite him in the same position, eager, excited, nervous. They were in a small room that was devoid of statues, paintings, rugs or anything else that might have given the room a special ambience. The only warmth came from a few flickering candles. Akash opened his eyes.

"You want to fly," the monk said.

"Yes."

Akash looked at Barnaby as if reading him. The staring continued for what seemed like a long time. At one point, Akash raised an eyebrow. At another, he frowned.

"You are not ready," he finally said.

He didn't say it unkindly, he simply relayed it as a fact. He had read Barnaby and had found that the man was not ready. Barnaby, struggling with his emotions, stared at the monk and Akash just sat there with infinite calm.

"My whole life," Barnaby said, "… every moment, every breath, every thought, every dream … I have never wanted anything else."

"Your mind is ready," Akash replied, leaning forward. "But your heart. Your heart not ready." Barnaby looked at the monk in confusion. "The woman outside," Akash explained.

"… No," Barnaby said, shaking his head. "There is nothing."

Akash fell silent again and read Barnaby once more.

Finally, he rose, his bones cracking. Taking a deep breath, the monk motioned for Barnaby to rise as well.

"We shall see," Akash said.

## EMBRACE EVERYTHING

Martha kept pacing, more anxious with every second Barnaby spent in there in the company of the old man. When the monastery door finally opened, Ram jumped to his feet. Martha watched as Barnaby followed Akash to the edge of the cliff to the stepping stone, a flat stone that jutted out into the void.

Akash's robe flowed with the wind and there was something dark and ominous about it. When he motioned for Barnaby to step forward, Martha ran.

Ram tried to hold her back but she shook him off and stepped between Barnaby and Akash.

"Barnaby, let's talk about this," she said, doing her best to sound calm, in control.

Trying to ignore her, Barnaby stepped around Martha to stand next to Akash, a foot from the dizzying drop.

Martha swallowed hard and moved forward to stand on Barnaby's other side.

"Let go of everything," Akash intoned.

"I'm right here," Martha said.

Barnaby tried to concentrate.

"Empty your mind," Akash continued. "Empty your heart."

"If you jump, you die," Martha said, both angry and desperate. "Look down, Barnaby, there were others."

"No fears," Akash said, his voice unchanged, humming. "No dreams. No memories."

"Sure, yes. Forget everything," Martha shot back, louder now. She kept addressing Barnaby as he looked straight out into void. "Forget Vanessa, forget Aura, forget Mr. Merlin and forget Bharad."

"Let go of hope. Of love. Let go of everything," the old monk said and even Martha had to fight the captivating sound of his voice. She suddenly realized that Barnaby was taking a step closer to the edge. She felt her tears as she cried out.

"Barnaby, please, no!"

He took another step.

"When everything is gone," Akash said, "you can fly."

Barnaby looked into the sky and looked down and there was no fear. And yet he frowned and then ... one step, just one step, he moved back. Barnaby looked from the monk to Martha.

"I don't want to let go," Barnaby said. "I don't want to be weightless."

Martha embraced him fiercely and Barnaby put his arms around her, too. In this embrace, he opened his eyes and saw Akash looking at him. To Barnaby's surprise, the monk smiled and lightly bowed.

"Now you are ready," Akash said.

Without another glance he returned into the monastery, followed by Ram. The boy monk, still looking gravely concerned, bowed to Barnaby and Martha before silently closing the door.

They were alone and Barnaby smiled at Martha. She felt more relieved than ever before. Everything would be all right.

"What are we going to do now?" she asked.

"I understand now, Martha."

"What?"

"It's not about letting go. It's about embracing it."

"What are you talking about?" Martha asked with growing concern.

"Everything, Martha. Everything."

Fear surged back into her as Barnaby walked to stand against the side of the mountain, twenty feet from the stepping stone. A quick run.

"What are you doing?" she said, alarmed.

"I'm going to fly," he said as if it were the obvious thing to do.

Martha felt the earth slip away from under her. As she stepped into his path, it all merged. Numbing fear turned into white-hot anger and furious desperation.

"Barnaby, it's impossible. Flying is impossible. That was nothing but a crazy old man, don't you see?!"

"I am ready," was all he replied.

"No. I'm not going to let you kill yourself. You will not jump. We are going to climb down this mountain. We will find our way back home and we will have a good life. A life, Barnaby, a life!"

He hugged her once more with all his might before stepping away from her.

"If you jump, I jump!" she yelled at him. "Do you hear me!? I will jump!"

Barnaby smiled at her with great affection.

"Barnaby, please," she said.

"Embrace everything," he said and sounded completely at peace, content with the world, content with life. Here. Now. Perfect. Excitement shining in his eyes, he pushed off from the rock and ran. Martha clasped her hands over her mouth.

He jumped off the stepping stone without hesitation, at full speed … and for just an instant Martha's heart surged with hope. For just one instant Barnaby seemed to be suspended in the air.

And then he fell out of sight.

Martha stared, eyes wide open, unblinking. She kept her eyes glued on the place where he had been moments before. Hoping that Barnaby would suddenly soar into view again, leap up, pirouette, laugh and soar higher.

What if, Martha, what if.

She sank to her knees and cried and screamed and the wind picked up and carried her scream into the sky, into the clouds and up to the birds.

# CHAPTER FOUR

## FREEDOM

# THE STORY OF CHARLES

He had always loved Martha. Always. When they were students it was new and often wild. There had been other girlfriends before her … but none after. It broke his heart when she went her own way, when she fell in love with John Lewis, when she got married. He kept in touch, loosely, always afraid his feelings would show. He was happy for her when she gave birth to a son and devastated when that son took his own life fifteen years later.

Out of concern he had stayed away from her … and out of concern he had kept an eye on her. He knew about her therapy, he knew about her difficulties coming to grips with her past and moving on. He knew about the alienation from her husband and when he left, Charles wanted to rush over and take her in his arms. He didn't. He respected her too much, gave her time and only called her six months later to suggest a position at St. Joseph's. He knew she needed structure and purpose and St. Joseph's would be able to give her that.

And yes, Charles would be able to be around her again.

Her time at the hospital was all but easy for Charles.

He kept his professional distance, at least for the most part, he thought. He saw her working hard, he saw her making a true difference. And, although he wouldn't have wished that patient on her, he saw the powerful sense of purpose Martha experienced when working with Barnaby Smith. He thought he would be able to control it, to guide her, to help her improve over time … the outlandish idea that Martha would kidnap her patient had never been a consideration.

~

Charles walked across the tarmac from the plane to the flat red-bricked building of Kathmandu airport. He took one slow step after another, following a few dozen other passengers, looked around and wistfully smiled when he saw the white mountains, rising in the distance against a clear blue sky.

He had time, all the time in the world. Charles thought back to the time after Martha's disappearance.

The attention had been enormous for a few days, headline after headline about the damaged psychiatrist who, with the aid of a nurse, had kidnapped a severely disturbed patient. But just as soon as the tabloids had picked up on the story, they moved on to the next. Charles had to endure a number of excruciating interviews with know-it-all reporters who clearly didn't care about any of the people involved. He handled his job as chief administrator of St. Joseph's well, came across as a consummate professional and actually came out strengthened in his position as the head of the facility. The newspapers tried to damage him but even their poking fun at his consistent bow tie appearances didn't stick. To the great dismay of Dr. Steward, Charles was seen as the man in charge, dealing professionally with a difficult situation.

In the months and years that followed, Steward continued on his quest to usurp Charles' position. He kept examining and reexamining the meetings between Charles and Martha and, most of all, between Martha and Barnaby. He laid out everything that he considered had gone wrong. He highlighted all the red flags that, according to him, Charles should have seen. It didn't work. Increasingly frustrated, Dr. Henry Steward eventually realized that he would never reach his goal, neither the one of Charles' position, nor the one of finding Martha Lewis and Barnaby Smith. He quit six years after the kidnapping and Charles had never heard from him since.

Where Steward had spent his time blustering, Charles had remained quiet – but was, at the same time, far more active. He diligently worked with the police. He regularly visited Martha's apartment to read her notes and to stare at that 'Barnaby wall' for hours on end. It didn't take investigators long to trace the last use of Martha's credit card to Mumbai. It took them a while longer to discover how Martha had managed to get there undetected. But that's where the trail ended. US authorities continued to work with their Indian counterparts, a taskforce was set up, information was exchanged but none of that information ever extended beyond Mumbai.

Charles knew about every step taken and kept his own file. And when, seven years after Martha's vanishing, the case was long cold, he still kept at it. Every day. He had two lives. One in his role at St. Joseph's, the other as private investigator with one single case to solve – to find Martha Lewis. When her apartment was emptied, Martha's former husband agreed to let Charles have all the files and notes and books pertaining to patient Barnaby Smith. Over time, Charles had pasted and pinned a 'Martha wall' in his own home. He loved sitting there, musing, looking at pictures of her, trying to understand her thinking, trying to map her path beyond Mumbai.

The big break came only after retirement. He had decided to follow up on every bit of information and flew to Mumbai to meet every single one of Bharad's cousins.

When he talked to a man named Ajay, when he looked into the man's eyes, he instantly knew that another bit of the Martha Lewis' mystery was about to be unveiled. Ajay had, in previous years, maintained that he had met them but that Bharad had died the day of his arrival in India.

According to Ajay the doctor and her patient had disappeared that day.

The meeting with Ajay so many years later revealed a different story that would led Charles to Nepal.

## MUST BE NICE UP THERE

Charles had a lot of time to think as he traveled first by car and eventually on the back of a mule. The journey tired him more than anything before, but although he expected another dead end, he found himself smiling a lot. He forgot to shave and liked the stubble. As he climbed into more and more remote mountain territory he realized that one thing hadn't changed – he continued wearing his bow tie.

As his eyes kept to the path, his mind wandered to Martha. For years, he had analyzed every facet of her and he believed he knew her better than anybody. He understood her. He could easily theorize about the reasons for her unorthodox actions. He could see why she had taken Barnaby, why she had needed to do it for him – and for herself. But one thing he could never put together. As flying was clearly impossible for human beings, Martha must have known that, at some point, pretense would fall. That moment had to come. For Barnaby, for her. What had she been hoping to do then?

Stop poking me, Charles thought.

He woke but the poking didn't stop until he opened his eyes. He'd fallen asleep on the mule. The old guide grinned a toothless smile and pointed.

A monastery, hidden away behind green slopes.

Charles climbed off the mule, his backside aching. He stretched and hoped he'd find another clue in that place. As the guide lay down outside the monastery, Charles decided to explore. The place seemed deserted. He walked through the peaceful grounds of the monastery.

Charles heard water, a nearby creek, perhaps. He heard birds, saw a few. But there were no people.

He found a temple that stood open and seemed to invite him. Without hesitation, Charles entered. In the murky light of the temple he found himself surrounded by statues, offerings and smoking incense sticks of various sizes and shapes.

On a whim, he took an incense stick and was about to light it when he noticed a monk's silhouette against the light coming from the entrance.

"I'm sorry," Charles said, feeling uncomfortable for speaking English, "I just wanted to light one of these for a friend."

"Anyone I know?" came the reply.

The monk stepped forward and Charles couldn't believe his eyes when he recognized Martha, dressed in an orange robe, her head shaved. She looked serene. As Charles gaped, she smiled.

"Hello, Charles," she simply said.

In a display most unlike himself, Charles ran forward and hugged her.

Martha put her arms around him and gave Charles all the time he needed. He suddenly broke the embrace, took a step back and adjusted his bow tie.

"I didn't mean to do that," he said. "No doubt inappropriate."

"I'm glad you did," Martha said with a wink.

She walked and motioned for him to follow her. Martha led him into the monastery's garden where several nuns were at work, tending flowers and vegetables.

You found her, Charles shouted on the inside, you found her! They walked next to each other, in silence, both of them smiling. Charles wasn't entirely sure he wasn't dreaming. But if he was, it was a dream he hoped to never wake from. The gardens, the majestic Himalayan mountains, blue skies with cotton clouds and birds weaving in and out. What a setting for a dream, Charles thought.

"It took you a while," Martha said.

"I didn't have a lot to go on," Charles replied.

"How are you?" Martha said, looking at him, examining his face.

"Good, good. Retired last year. Lots of time on my hands," Charles said. Martha smiled at him as she stopped to show a young nun how to best harvest herbs. "How long have you been here, Martha?"

"Nine years."

"Like it?" Charles asked and knew the answer when

she smiled, just smiled. "You look happy."

"I am."

She stopped at a little creek, picked up water with her hands and drank. She offered water to Charles and he drank from her hands. As they stood there, a lark landed next to them. It drank, looked at them, drank again and flew up. Charles' eyes followed the bird.

"I like this place," he said.

"We have guest rooms," Martha said.

And with that, Charles knew that he would stay there. If not with her, at the very least near her. He hadn't been happier in years. This was good.

His eyes kept following the lark as it rose higher and higher.

"About Barnaby," he said.

"Yes?"

"What happened?" Charles asked.

"He flew," she replied.

The lark crossed paths with other birds and Charles saw them flying in and out of clouds.

Squinting his eyes, he saw another bird, lazily circling way up there.

Must be a big bird, Charles thought.

Must be nice up there.

# THE FARMER SMILES

Embrace everything. Those had been Barnaby's words. Good words, words to live by and Martha had done just that from that day forward. And now Charles was here. She had a feeling he would stay. And she embraced the idea as she embraced the glow of the morning sun and the sting of the wasp. Life was good.

Martha felt at peace. Some might have called her wise and she would have smiled at that notion. She knew nothing. She knew everything.

Her hand brushed across Barnaby's diary. It lay in its special spot on Martha's one shelf. Years ago she would read his words, she would search them, drown in them – and sometimes she would speak his thoughts out loud. And then one day she simply stopped and allowed those words to slide into the past. Barnaby's diary remained, a silent companion in her room. A gift she had received a long time ago.

Standing in her small, white-washed room, she opened the window as she did every evening. It was early evening, the light still clear across the mountains, across the hills and valleys below.

There was so much she wanted to tell Charles, so

much she would tell him. In time. She had given Charles a tour of the monastery, had introduced him to everyone there. And, after a light meal, she had shown him his room. It was the one reserved for guests, large and nicely furnished, and Charles loved it. He seemed to have planned what he did next. As if he'd always told himself that, if he found Martha, he would do just that. In almost ceremonious fashion he had taken off his bow tie.

Yes, she would tell Charles everything.

The view from her window was magnificent. Some of the mountain peaks were still aglow in the rays of the setting sun. Twilight was falling over the green hills below. Martha saw the winding path, leading up to the monastery. She saw the village in the valley and she saw a farmer's solitary hut on the hill across.

In the waning light, Martha looked at the small house, a farm like any other in these parts, with just a few narrow fields, carved like steps into the side of the hill, leading to the house on top.

Martha spotted the farmer as he left the goat shed. The man walked past the vegetable patch toward the house, his fingers brushing past bushes and leaves.

There was an elegance to the farmer's walk, as if the cracks in the ground, the hardened clumps of soil and the rocks, didn't apply to his feet.

Birds were there, many birds, on the roof of his house and circling around and above the farmer.

He did what he always did. He stopped, that same moment, that same place. Martha saw his face as if he were standing next to her.

They looked at each from other across the valley and both raised their hands in greeting.

Martha cherished this moment of warmth, of clarity. Life is simple.

The farmer lifted his face to the sky and spread his arms.

And he smiled.

## THE END

# ALSO BY THIS AUTHOR

## THE CHAMP

At the tender age of one hundred and fifteen, Wilber Patorkin he's the oldest man alive in the United States of America, the champion of age. His body is failing him gloriously, his legs will barely carry him, his quivering lips and dentures turn his words into meaningless babble... and yet he has the clearest brain and the brightest eyes you'll ever come across. His steps may be tiny, but his story is epic. His words may be few, but his mind goes beyond your wildest imagination. Join Wilber on a most unlikely journey and be prepared - you just may discover yourself along the way.

What reviewers write: *"Eckhart has created a wonderfully warm and eccentric main character in 115-year-old Wilber Patorkin."* – *"A story of friendship, mortality, and good vs. evil, it was so good I couldn't put it down."* – *"A crossover between Amélie Poulain and Benjamin Button."* – *"The style is a compelling mix between Stephen King & JD Salinger."*

# HOME

When eighty-two-year-old Max Flynn meets Wal. Miller, he can't believe his eyes. Walt is not only seven and a half feet tall, he also looks exactly like the giant Max knew as a child during Coney Island's golden years. Max, a former cop who spent his life protecting the island and the people walking upon it, decides to solve the mystery of 'the impossible man'. As Max learns more and more about Walt Miller, he finds friendship, love, a dark secret and a world beyond his wildest dreams.

This is a novel about home, about the earth, about the land we walk on. This is also a novel about being mindful and doing the right thing. In Walt's words: "Max Flynn gives me hope. There must be others like him. People who care deeply, deeply enough to hear the heartbeat of the land they walk on. They are the future. They will be the balance."

What reviewers write: *"The heart truly is where Home is."* – *"It made me cry and left me feeling new, forever young and hopeful."* – *"Imaginative, life affirming and magical."* – *"The perfect recipe for a heartwarming book."* – *"This just has to be made into a movie."*

# TALES OF WYCHWOOD

.e many special places in the world, places rich
.story and legend, blood and life, love and death.
.l of those many places, none is more special than
.hwood Forest. Wychwood, the small remnant of a
.rest that has once spanned the width of England, is far
more than your average woods - it is a prison that holds
fierce warrior elves, bloodthirsty headhunter dwarves and
darker creatures, still. For hundreds of years a family of
humans has helped the elves to protect the forest and
those who roam within. Tales of Wychwood is the story
of a one-of-a-kind grandmother and her grandchildren,
who are about to discover everything about their glorious
secret ancestry. Join Nick, Milo and Ellie as they enter a
fantastical world filled with deadly dangers, high
adventure and darkest mystery.

*What reviewers write: "The forest of Wychwood had me in its
clutches within the first few pages. Energizing, liberating, magical...
enchanting!" – "Having lived in and around the forest for 30 years,
this book does not ease the fears the ancient woodland screams at
you. If you lived here you would read this in a different light. If you
don't then you will want to visit."*

# ABOUT THE AUTHOR

Daniel Martin Eckhart is a screenwriter and a novelist. Many moons ago, long before discovering his love for storytelling, he guarded the life of the Pope in the Vatican, worked for the United Nations in Israel, Lebanon, Iraq and Iran and studied acting in New York at the glorious Neighborhood Playhouse School of the Theatre.

These days the author lives on a 17th century farm in Switzerland together with his wife, three children, a monster dog and a psychotic cat.

Printed in Great Britain
by Amazon